Almost Hollywood

The Forgotten Story of Jacksonville, Florida

Blair Miller

HAMILTON BOOKS

A member of
THE ROWMAN & LITTLEFIELD PUBLISHING GROUP
Lanham • Boulder • New York • Toronto • Plymouth, UK

Copyright © 2013 by
Hamilton Books
4501 Forbes Boulevard
Suite 200
Lanham, Maryland 20706
Hamilton Books Acquisitions Department (301) 459-3366

10 Thornbury Road
Plymouth PL6 7PP
United Kingdom

All rights reserved

British Library Cataloging in Publication Information Available

Library of Congress Control Number: 2012948324
ISBN: 978-0-7618-5995-6

Contents

List of Figures		v
Foreword		vii
Acknowledgments		ix
Introduction		1
Timeline		12
1	Mayor Bowden, Politics, and the Movie Industry	14
2	Kalem Company, Inc.	28
3	Lubin Motion Picture Company	40
4	Vim Comedy Company	45
5	Amber Star Company and the Eastern Film Company	57
6	King-Bee Film Corporation	60
7	Eagle Film Company	67
8	Thanhouser Company	74
9	Klever Pictures, Inc.	95
10	Klutho Studios	100
11	Other Studios	104

12 What Happened to the Dream of Making Jacksonville into
What Hollywood, California, Ultimately Became? 112

Bibliography 128

Index 133

List of Figures

I.1.	The Call of Jacksonville	2
I.2.	J.B. Pound Hotel Chain	8
I.3.	Hotel Seminole, Jacksonville, Florida	9
1.1.	Hotel Mason, Jacksonville, Florida	17
1.2.	Windsor Hotel, Jacksonville, Florida	24
1.3.	Windsor Hotel, Jacksonville, Florida	24
1.4.	Windsor Hotel, Jacksonville, Florida	25
2.1.	Roseland Hotel	33
2.2.	Roseland Hotel	33
2.3.	Comedian Team of Ham and Bud (Kalem)	34
2.4.	Mabel Normand in the film Sis Hopkins	37
4.1.	Oliver Hardy & Kate Price of the Vim Comedy Company	48
4.2.	Pearl Bailey, Budd Ross, "Babe" Oliver Hardy, Ethel Burton, 1916	48
4.3.	Kate Price, Actress for Vim Studios	49
4.4.	The Moving Picture World, April 1, 1916	49
4.5.	Comedians Burns & Stull	50
4.6.	Comedians Burns & Stull	50
4.7.	Comedians Burns & Stull	51
4.8.	Rosemary Theby	53
4.9.	Harry Myers	53
6.1.	Arvid Gillstrom with Ethel Burton Palmer	61
6.2.	King Bee—Billy West Advertisement	63
6.3.	King Bee Film Corporation—Billy West Advertisement	64
6.4.	King Bee Film Corporation—Billy West Advertisement	65
8.1.	Thanhouser Film Corporation Headquarters, Jacksonville, Florida	75

8.2.	Walter Hiers, Thanhouser Company	80
8.3.	Riley Chamberline, Comedian, Thanhouser Company	80
8.4.	Falstaff Comedies, Thanhouser Company	81
9.1.	Victor Moore, Principal Comedian, Klever Komedies	97
10.1.	Klutho Studios — Interior and Exterior Stages	101
10.2.	Klutho Studios — Interior Stage	101
11.1.	Dixieland Theatre, Dixieland Park, Jacksonville, Florida	105
11.2.	Café and Dancing Pavilion, Dixieland Park, Jacksonville, Florida	105
11.3.	Dixieland Park, Jacksonville, Florida	106
11.4.	Entrance to Ostrich Farm, Jacksonville, Florida	106
11.5.	Ostrich Farm, Jacksonville, Florida	107
11.6.	At the Ostrich Farm, Jacksonville, Florida	107

Foreword

Ned Thanhouser

I have a personal connection with Jacksonville. My grandparents, Edwin and Gertrude Thanhouser, along with brother-in-law Lloyd Lonergan, established the Thanhouser Company in 1909 in New Rochelle, New York, to capitalize on the transition of mass entertainment from theatre to motion pictures. From 1910 to 1917, Thanhouser produced and released over 1,000 silent films that went into worldwide distribution. The films were a blend of classic tales, combined with mysteries, dramas, and light comedy. In January 1912, Thanhouser sent a company of actors, a director, a stage manager and a cameraman to Jacksonville for two months where they made about 20 films.

By 1915, motion pictures had become the third largest industry in the US behind oil and automobiles. It was only natural that the burgeoning moving picture industry founded in the Northeastern United States would expand beyond is roots to Jacksonville to take advantage of its warm climate, excellent rail access, and the lack of tourists (most visited Miami by this time) meant prices and labor were cheap.

Jacksonville had now earned the title of the "Winter Film Capital of the World" and was home to over 30 studios employing thousands of actors, directors, cameramen and studio employees. In December 1915, Thanhouser expanded operations to Jacksonville by building a permanent studio at a cost of $30,000 where it produced dozens of films, mostly comedies marketed under the Thanhouser Falstaff brand.

Jacksonville city government officials, lead by Mayor J.E.T. Bowden, actively worked to seize the opportunity to establish the city as a permanent base of operations for US and international film corporations. The future of the film industry in Jacksonville was looking very bright, or so it would seem.

In May 1916, however, Thanhouser shuttered its Jacksonville studio with a promise to reopen in September, but this never happened. And by the end of 1917 Jacksonville became a "ghost town" as far as motion picture productions were concerned.

What caused this abrupt reversal of fortune forcing the film industry out of Jacksonville and to Hollywood?

To answer this question, Blair Miller has resurrected the forgotten story of the rise and fall of the motion picture industry in Jacksonville. He provides us with a compelling view into the intriguing political climate, social issues, and global events that contributed to Jacksonville's meteoric rise and fall that took place in just a few short years. Through painstaking research, compilation of contemporary news articles and personal research in Jacksonville's archives, he reveals this story by recounting the history of dozen or so studios, including Thanhouser, which bet on Jacksonville as the next Mecca for filmmaking while weaving through it the political maneuverings of civic leaders who forfeited Jacksonville's chance at becoming what we know today as Hollywood.

—Portland, Oregon (November, 2005)

Acknowledgments

The author gratefully acknowledges the assistance of my research assistant Carol K. Farrell, in obtaining the information necessary to complete this manuscript. Without your help, Mom, I would never have had the financial means or ability to return to Jacksonville a second time for the additional information needed to complete this book manuscript.

This manuscript would be lacking if it did not include mention of the primary first hand knowledge source of information used in this book. The Florida Room, Jacksonville's main public library, is an entry point to the early 1900's film history of Jacksonville. Its staff is a treasure to any researcher needing to use its facility and resources. I am indebted to them for their help. By using the early issues of the Florida Times-Union and Metropolis newspapers, and having specific articles to access, it was possible to recreate over time important elements of the film history. Even though this book covers only a limited number of the reported 30 film companies thought to be filming in Jacksonville in 1916, it is thought to be sufficient to describe the circumstances. It remains for some other writer to document other studios that operated there.

I am also extremely fortunate to have benefited from the excellent CD-ROM disc Thanhouser Films: An Encyclopedia and History, 1909-1918, by Q. David Bowers. It was obtained from Ned Thanhouser and the Thanhouser Company Film Preservation Inc., in Portland, Oregon. Mr. Thanhouser has been very helpful to me, and I am indeed fortunate to have had him review the manuscript and write a foreword for it.

Thanks also are extended to a number of friends who helped. Sven Ahrenkilde helped with the photographs in the book. Using Photoshop and scanning it was possible to scan postcard images and then print them as photographs that appear within this book. Frederick Clyve Britton helped by doing a final editing of the manuscript. Kristine Krueger, of the National Film Information Service at the Margaret Herrick Library Center for Motion Picture Study, provided valuable background information. Raymond W. Neal, Librarian Senior, Florida Collection, Jacksonville Pubic Library, helped by providing prints of picture postcards from the library collection. Robert T. Silkett, a Florida Collection librarian, provided encouragement and information by email when it was most needed.

Finally, I would be remiss not to credit certain books that have preceded this one, from which I gathered nuggets of factual knowledge about the subject matter. It is gratifying to realize that I have brought together information from many different sources, hopefully resulting in a better overall understanding of the role that the city of Jacksonville played in the history of the cinema.

Introduction

As we cackle joyously at home at the pranks of our children, recalling similar pranks of our own childhood, we laugh at the film comedies. Not so much because they are funny in themselves, as because they take us out of ourselves, ease us out of the restrictions that care would put upon us, and take us again to the days of our childhood, when all the world was carefree and happy.

The antics of the film comedians amuse us because they touch our memories of days forgotten. We laugh as much because of the days when we essayed similar pranks, as for the actual comedy portrayed on the screen.

It is our privilege to laugh at the fat ones, the skinny ones, the comic ones, and the tricks they employ to produce our laughter. They thrive upon our appreciation in increased prestige and salary, and we thrive on our laughter in increased digestion and a more wholesome outlook upon life in general.

(Film Flashes: The Wit and Humor of a Nation in Pictures, Leslie-Judge Company, 1916)

Before Hollywood, early motion picture companies came to Florida—taking advantage of the sunny days and good weather to maximize outdoor filming time. Good weather, for outdoor filming, was a far greater uncertainty in the area around New York City and New Jersey—where filmmaking had previously been centered.

Jacksonville, Florida became known as "the World's Winter Film Capital" and was home to a number of silent film comedy companies. Vim Comedy Company, Amber-Star Studios, Eagle Film Manufacturing and Production Company, King-Bee Films Corporation, Klever Pictures, Inc., Lubin Manufacturing Company, Kalem Comedies, Klutho Studios, Thanhouser comedies—all established a filmmaking presence in Jacksonville. Additional studios—such as Edison, Gaumont, Essanay, Vitagraph and Biograph—also

The Call of Jacksonville

BY WALTER R. EARLY

JACKSONVILLE, FLORIDA, has convinced motion picture producers of its advantages for film making. It is said that a producer can work at least two hours longer each day in Jacksonville than he could at any other point in the United States. Conditions are ideal.

The southern metropolis now houses studios of the following companies: Gaumont, Kalem, Vim, Eagle, Thanhouser and Palm.

The following concerns are negotiating with a view of making Jacksonville their winter headquarters: Metro, Columbia, Peerless, World and Ocean.

Every property owner in the city is said to be in favor of encouraging film manufacturers to locate there. Resolutions to this effect have been passed by the Board of Trade, Chamber of Commerce, Tourist and Convention Bureaus, the Rotary Club, the Real Estate Exchange and other prominent civic organizations. Most of the citizens have agreed to donate gratis any locations the motion picture men may select.

Twelve furniture stores have announced that they will rent at a reasonable figure any kind of furniture, office fixtures or other necessities listed under "props." City officials have gone on record as welcoming producers to Jacksonville. They have gone so far as to send plain clothes policemen with directors to see that the streets are cleared in order that there will be no interference with them in their work.

Jacksonville offers an abundance of locations. The city has buildings of the latest designs. Some of them are fifteen stories in height. The hotels are equal to any in the land, furnished modern in every respect. The hotel proprietors are willing to hand over the keys to the motion picture men. They permit the screen workers to use the interiors for any kind of a scene.

In the immediate vicinity of Jacksonville, there is nearly any kind of an out-door location. One of the finest bathing beaches in the world is only eighteen miles from the city. Twenty minutes separates the city from a first-class jungle. Farm scenes are everywhere. The St. Johns river offers boats and steamships of ever description.

The Florida Ostrich farm, with more than 200 birds and a large number of animals, is available at any time. The alligator section of the farm, with nearly 2,000 of the reptiles, offers wide possibilities for the director.

Occasionally mountains are necessitated by scenarios. While Florida is considered a level state, there is, a short distance from Jacksonville, locations that would delight the most skeptical producer.

Some have expressed a fear that summer in Florida is one degree short of Hades. The writer has spent many summers in Florida. Of course, it is hot. But even in July and August, it is not hot enough to cause sunstroke, nor has it been known that any one was overcome by the heat in any part of this country. The nights are cool and after an exhausting day's work, one may retire to enjoy as refreshing a sleep as though one was near the North Pole, taking everything into consideration.

All in all, there seems to be no place in the United States that offers the inducements to motion picture producers as this wonderful city of Jacksonville. The man who has never visited the city cannot appreciate the meaning of the word "co-operation." Once he comes, Jacksonville will be satisfied to leave her case in his hands.

An important feature about this section of the country is the fact that Jacksonville is only a matter of twenty-six hours from New York City and thirty hours from Chicago. A director may leave his home office in either of the cities mentioned late Saturday night and start work in the southern metropolis Monday morning. He may finish his picture in one week and be back home the following Monday.

There are firms here that do developing and printing, rent studios and out-door stages for the use of companies merely paying the city a visit.

The rays of the sun permit the producer to be on the job early in the morning and late in the evening. Weather conditions are ideal.

Figure I.1. The Call of Jacksonville (Motography Trade Publication).

filmed here on a more limited basis. By 1916, there were 30 companies filming in Jacksonville. The focus of this book is focused solely on the companies that made comedy films.

Material for this book is drawn largely from local period newspaper sources. The *Florida Times Union* newspapers, and the *Sunday Metropolis*, from turn of the century Jacksonville, have been preserved on microfilm at the Hayden Burns Library in Jacksonville. Where appropriate the book will include direct quotes from these newspaper articles—allowing the reader to gain an appreciation for how the movie company people thought, acted and interacted with the early residents of Jacksonville. Facts upon which this book is based are also drawn from these newspapers.

Additional information is from the Margaret Herrick Library, in Los Angeles, California. In this regard the assistance of Kristine Krueger has proved of enormous value in supplementing my research, which has culminated in this manuscript.

Books consulted for factual information have supplemented the above materials.

What this book seeks to do is focus on the comedy films made in Jacksonville, and yet place the comedy filmmaking within the larger context of political and social developments and reactions to the overall subject of filmmaking in Jacksonville. Not everyone in Jacksonville was in favor of the film industry that located there. It remains for a future researcher to explore the rest of Jacksonville's filmmaking manifestations.

This book is seen as a companion volume to the author's *American Silent Film Comedies: An Illustrated Encyclopedia of Persons, Studios and Terminology* (McFarland, 1995). However, while *American Silent Film Comedies* was organized in an encyclopedic format, this book is organized in a more conventional chapter format.

The narrowed focus, of the present volume, allows a more detailed accounting of comedy filmmaking in Jacksonville than was either possible or appropriate in the author's 1995 book. Included is a full and complete index and a filmography of comedies made by each studio. Separate chapters deal with:

- Individual movie companies including pertinent information about the comedians and comediennes, producers, directors and cameramen who worked at each.
- Discussion of how the residents of Jacksonville reacted to the arrival of movie people in their city.
- *Why Florida in general and specifically Jacksonville never was able to become the Hollywood of the South and the movie industry eventually settled in California.

Why did Jacksonville become home to the early film industry? The answer lies in a combination of factors. First, Jacksonville was a major stop on the vaudeville circuits that included major cities such as Chicago and Philadelphia. It was also a winter home for vaudeville performers and thus became known to the film industry when vaudeville people started to become associated with the newly emerging film industry. Secondly, Jacksonville and the surrounding area offered a variety of settings for filmmakers—and the weather that was usually more dependable for filming than in New York, New Jersey and other northern filming locations. Finally, being located on the shore of the St. John's River made it relatively easy to ship equipment, sets, costumes etc. from New York City to the various Jacksonville studios. The presence of railroad tracks all the way to New York City was also of importance.

Filmmaking in Jacksonville provided a big boost to the local economy, and a variety of businesses. Local citizens and politicians stood ready to welcome and encourage the film industry to locate here. In a *Florida Metropolis* (January 23, 1916, page 4B) article entitled "Other Industries Will Follow the Movies to Jax," journalist Walter R. Early emphasizes how the movie companies helped the local economy . . .

> Much has been written about the value to the city of Jacksonville to secure as many moving picture producing concerns as possible, but nothing has been said about the other lines of business and the many people, other than those who are actually working in the films who will come here on account to the picture makers being here, and the half has not been told as to the actual amount of money that will be spent here, once the majority of producers locate in this vicinity.
>
> Instead of the annual pay rolls of the film companies being $20,000.00 it is several times that amount, if the number of working men and women are included who do not, as a rule, appear in the pictures. The amount of money, spent for accessories, such as lumber, costumes, wigs, canvas, scenic artists, furniture, general house and other furnishings, as in the making of pictures, every conceivable sort of thing is used: in a great many instances the thing that to the layman is of least importance, to the producer becomes an absolute necessity: many cast off wagons, old shacks of houses, broken down automobiles and things of a like nature are used to lend the proper atmosphere to a picture. All of these things come up at a time least expected.
>
> Few, if any, moving picture producing companies can get along with less than a thousand dollars a week expenses, and if there are any who get along with as small a weekly outlay as that, the writer does not know of them, while the average company will easily spend from $2,000 a week to $10,000. Right here in Jacksonville the Vim Company, whose studios are on Riverside Avenue, spend an average of $1,000 per week.

The Thanhouser Film Corporation, who have built a studio on Eighth Street, near Main, are spending as much as $6,000 each week.

The Gaumont Film Company, who are working in South Jacksonville, spends at least $5,000 a week, and the Kalem Company, who have been making pictures here for the last seven years, averages $300,000 a year.

The Metro Film Corporation, with their eight producing companies, will easily spend $25,000 a week, and the Paramount Program will go as much as $3,000 a week. The Equitable Film Company spent fully as much as the Metro, and one might go indefinitely about the amount each company spends in making pictures. With the coming of the producer to this or any city, it means a following of allied interests, such as costumers, wig makers, carpenters, property makers, electricians, to say nothing of the large number of extra people who work occasionally in the films, many of whom earn more 'jobbing' than they could were they to follow other vocations.

All of these people mean more money spent here, as they will have to find homes or hotels or boarding houses and in case it means just that much more from every angle.

The establishment of property shops means the employment of several local people in each instance, while the costumer will often get a call for several hundred suits of a certain kind. This means work day and night in order to make them right here, and will call for a large number of women who can sew and work on such things. In the case of the carpenter shops, nearly every scene will have to be built especially for whatever picture that might be in the making and the company will, as a rule, carry their own men for such work, but they also have to bring or engage locally a property man who can do the borrowing of furniture and other small things that may have to be used, but will not pay to have built.

The scenic artist is a most important personage as it is he who paints the set that the carpenter built and the property man decorated and furnished. These are all big salaried men as compared to men of commercial life, as very few of them as individuals draw less than $40 a week, and some several times that amount, especially the scenic artist. Then all the producers will sue laborers, and they pay them good wages, all of which will use up a lot of the unemployed men of the city. In the making of mob scenes the scenario sometimes calls for thousands of people and horses, steamships, railroad trains, etc.

All of these things have to be provided and cost lots of money. . . . The moving picture trade journals will send representatives here to look after their interests, all of which means unlimited advertising for Jacksonville and Florida, all of which hinges directly on to the picture makers.

The important thing right now is to get them to come here. . . . In every case the producer wants to work unhindered and when necessary ask for a little cooperation. If a director calls at your house and asks to be permitted to use your lawn or make a picture of the front or the inside of the building, let them do it freely: they will never do it the least bit of damage without paying for it. They, as a rule, leave your property just as they find it. If they call at your store to buy an article or a lot of goods, do not think for a minute that they do not know the actual value of what they want, and one of the best means of driving them out of a locality is to start boosting prices on the things they want.

Once this city takes its proper place as a film-producing center the general public will come in contact with the ones who work in the 'movies' and their favorite star will often be seen on the streets...and it is just as rude to stare them out of countenance as it is to do so in your own home. If the public will just let them come and go the same as ordinary people they will be conferring a greater favor than anything they can do.

The city also established a movie bureau to help film companies with their filmmaking needs. George A. Grimmer, Thanhouser's studio manager, in the June 4, 1916 (page 8) issue of the *Sunday Metropolis*, notes that ". . . The motion picture bureau helps the producer by securing all the extras, the necessary props, the best and most suitable locations and does away with large crowds of people hanging around the studio during the working hours looking for jobs."

Yet another perspective of how Jacksonville reacted to the movie people is provided in this article from page 5 of the June 11, 1916 issue of the *Sunday Metropolis* . . .

As most of the pictures are made on outdoor stages—with the sunlight diffused through a thin white sheet, which covers the entire stage so as to have no shadows—this permits of longer working hours for the companies. Being nearer New York, where practically all film releases are made, adds another advantage to Jacksonville, especially over the western points that possess somewhat similar climatic conditions, while the occasional boat trips that the companies make to New York permit them to take a variety of scenes which they could not otherwise obtain.

The advent of this industry in Jacksonville, with its army of workers, is especially welcomed by the merchants and businessmen of the city, for Jacksonville depends largely upon comparatively small and varied manufacturing industries to uphold its commercial life. Each producing company has from fifty to eighty people on its regular payroll, besides numerous 'extras' from time to time, making the combined pay rolls for all the companies amount to amount to about $10,000 per week, which means considerable new life injected into the trade arteries of the city.

The influx of the 'movie artists' has an appreciable effect upon the community immediately surrounding the location to a studio. Each company requires an area usually of several acres in which to arrange offices, store equipment, improvise stages, and various other necessities, consequently the studios are located in some uncrowded section of the city, most of them being on or near the banks of the river. As soon as necessary buildings, etc., are ready and the company is in full operation, this section of the city, which formerly was quiet and listless, suddenly takes on an air of activity and importance, making in all an appreciable improvement in the section.

Jacksonville's *Sunday Metropolis.* newspaper, in an article written for the June 14, 1916 issue (page 5) made clear how the community encouraged the film companies to locate in the city.

> Jacksonville will offer many inducements to the producer of motion pictures to come to this city this fall and settle permanently, but these inducements will not be in any way 'financial' or rather that is the way it looks now. They will be principally 'the good will of our people,' the hearty cooperation of our municipal government, the right hand of fellowship by the Jacksonville Chamber of Commerce, and the 'unexceeded atmosphere' of our hotels.
>
> The motion picture producer of importance does not need 'financial' aid, such as could be given him here, all he needs is what has been said above, and with this 'to be let alone,' he will make 'movies' and prosper, and the citizens of this city from the richest to the poorest will prosper with him.
>
> In speaking of inducements offered the producers, the first includes the idea that the citizens of this city 'must not look on the motion picture player as an alien,' but as an artist and one of us. We have had several hundred film artists in our midst since last November, and although many people looked askance at them at first, they soon won their way to our hearts and this confidence has none of them violated.
>
> The second inducement means the help of our mayor and city officials. Laws have been passed benefiting the producer in this city, and also protecting him, and every motion picture director or player who has visited this city has become a 'booster.'
>
> The third inducement is the help of the principal civic organization, the Jacksonville Chamber of Commerce, with some 2,200 live members. Whenever 'locations' are wanted, this body will gladly find them, and their fees are only the 'good will' of the producer. Its secretary, George E. Leonard, has been one of the most active citizens of this city in inducing the movies to locate here, and it is through the Chamber of Commerce that several of the studios we have now were secured.
>
> The fourth, last but not least inducement is that of our hostelries. The movie player is like other artists, he likes to gather at some favorite spot and mingle with fellow members of the profession, but there must be some sort of amusement provided for him, other than that which he can and will make. Jacksonville's finest hotels excel in furnishing amusement for the pleasure lovers, and most any night one may stroll to the Mason and find his or her friend listening to the strains of perfect music in the beautiful Japanese roof garden. Or to the Seminole, where the light fantastic is being indulged, in the handsome marble dining room, or to the Windsor, where the music of falling waters in the fountain room mingle with that of a superb orchestra.
>
> These are not the only pleasure providing spots, however. There are the several clubs in and around the city, and the beautiful Atlantic Beach Hotel

Figure I.2. J.B. Pound Hotel Chain (Blair Miller Collection).

Figure I.3. Hotel Seminole, Jacksonville, Florida (Blair Miller Collection).

at Atlantic Beach, where thousands annually seek the cool waters of the briny deep, and enjoys the pleasures of pulling their favorite ember of the piscatorial tribe from its placid depth.

There are inducements offered the player, producer, owner and cameraman, the later who is one of the most insistent that conditions be perfect from all sides and angles. We offer Mr. Cameraman the best climate in the world conductive to the filming of motion pictures. Hours unlimited, and atmosphere better than the best. Any cameraman who has ever 'filmed' a picture in this city will verify this, and we quote from such authorities as Jim Carleton, Lawrence Williams, Billy Sullivan, Jack Collins, Al Moses, George K. Hollister and Harry Keepers.

Take it all in all, where is there an Arcadia other than Jacksonville in the movie world? We are twenty-four hours from Broadway—think of it—only twenty-four hours from the center of the world, when it is 20 below zero, we are dipping daily in the beautiful ocean.

Efforts to attract motion picture companies to Jacksonville were spearheaded in no small way by the efforts of Jacksonville Mayor J.E.T. Bowden. In an open letter, in the *Sunday Metropolis*, dated January 22, 1916, Bowden extended an open invitation to motion picture producers to locate in Jacksonville. . . .

I, J.E.T. Bowden, as Mayor of the City of Jacksonville, Fla., do hereby extend a hearty invitation to the Motion Picture Producers, to make this city their center of production, assuring them a hearty welcome and every co-operation in facilitating their work.

Climatic conditions here make it possible for producers to work the entire year in comfort; we have every possible kind of location, either in the city or very close by, including tropical scenery and that of the pine-forest of the North. Our morning sun permits a longer working day than any other part of the country. We are only twenty-six hours from New York, the releasing center of the world.

And in coming to Jacksonville the Motion Picture people may rest assured that every reasonable assistance will be given in making their stay in the Land of Sunshine and Opportunity the most pleasant in the world. If in doubt, just ask those who are now here.

On the same page similar encouraging letters were contributed by H.H. Richardson, General Manager of the Jacksonville Tourist and Convention Bureau; Cilas A. Brown, Jr., president of the Jacksonville Real Estate Board; Charles H. Mann, president of the Jacksonville Chamber of Commerce; George E. Leonard, President of the Jacksonville Rotary Club; R.H. May, President of the Traffic Club and F.O. Miller, President of the State Good Roads Association.

The year 1916 was a good one for the motion picture business in Jacksonville. The December 12, 1916 issue, of the *Florida Metropolis* newspaper (page 3), reflected on this growth in the following words.

In the short space of a couple of years the city of Jacksonville has assumed the position of one of the leading centers for one of the youngest, though one of the greatest industries of the day.

Jacksonville today occupies in the South the same position that Los Angeles does in the West. Time was when the motion picture folks didn't know the South as a favorable and permanent location for the manufacture of films for the movie theaters. Los Angeles and other California cities commanded all the attention. But, gradually the people who are making the motion picture a great business it already is, and will be, have been attracted to Jacksonville, and the *Florida Metropolis* has continued to grow in the estimation of the movie world until today it commands a very high position...

Several years ago Jacksonville had only one or two studios and a handful of men and women in the business. Today the studios reach over a score, and the employees of the different studios aggregate into the hundreds. The payroll weekly amounts to many thousands of dollars.

The *Metropolis* sincerely believes that the next several years will see even more rapid strides in the development of this great industry. We want to call them home folks. We want them with us for many reasons, and Jacksonville should and will encourage them in every way possible.

Such was the climate of opinion in Jacksonville, which sought to encourage the film industry, in every way they could think of, to make the city a film capital. It is hoped that, within the context of this book, the reader will find the story of silent film comedies, in Jacksonville, as interesting to read as it was for me to write.

Timeline

1901   Fire destroys most of downtown Jacksonville. It is rebuilt and Jacksonville remains Florida's largest city until 1920. (*Lights! Camera! Florida*)

1908   (Sept. 9) The Motion Picture Patents Corporation is formed by Thomas Edison and the American Muto scope and Biograph Company. It became known simply as the "Patent Trust."

1910   Motion Picture Distributing and Sales Corporation is started by Mark Dintenfass, Charles Baumann and Carl Laemmle to oppose the "Patent Trust."

1912   (Sept.) In Edendale, California the Keystone Comedy Film Company is formed.

1913   At Keystone Studio Charlie Chaplin and Chester Conklin start making comedies, and in Jacksonville, Florida Oliver Hardy begins his film career at the Lubin Motion Pictures Company.

1914   (April 6) America officially enters World War I, 1914-1918.

1915   Jacksonville becomes known as the "World's Winter Film Capital."

William Fox starts the Fox Film Corporation. Also George K. Spoor and "Broncho Billy" Anderson start the Essanay Studios. Triangle-Keystone Film Company is formed.

(February 13) Lubin closes Jacksonville studio and leases the premises to Ocean Film Company. Subsequently Ocean goes bankrupt, leaving the way clear for Vim to lease the studio space. Patent Trust is disbanded by court order.

Thanhouser Film Corporation and Eagle Film Company build their studios in Jacksonville.

(August) Vitagraph buys all assets of Lubin's studio in Jacksonville. Out of business in Jacksonville Lubin unites with Vitagraph, Selig and Essanay to become V-L-S-E.

(November) Vim Comedy Company leases old Lubin studio, in Riverside section of Jacksonville. Louis Burstein and Mark Dintenfass own the company jointly. Prior to this (early fall), according to Rob Stone in *Laurel or Hardy*, Vim had made comedies at the vacated Centaur studio in Bayonne, New Jersey.

1916 Fernandez Perez appears in Vin comedies as Mr. Bungles. That same year he would appear in Eagle comedies as Tweedledum. His wife, Babette, played Tweedledee.

In California, the Lone Star Studio is established by Mutual Film Corporation as a site for Charlie Chaplin to make comedies. Located at 1025 Lillian Way, Hollywood.

Vitagraph buys the Kalem studios and forms Greater Vitagraph Company by merging itself with the Lubin, Selig and Essanay companies.

1917 Vim Comedy Company studio closes its doors due to mismanagement of company finances.

1922 In Jacksonville, Klutho studio goes out of business. Scandals in Hollywood.

Chapter One

Mayor Bowden, Politics, and the Movie Industry

In 1916 the future appeared bright for the movie industry in Jacksonville. There were some 30 studios operating in the city. The movie industry in Los Angeles was being criticized by the studios there for regulations and censorship that adversely affected the activities and operations of the studios. Support for the movie industry in New York City was waning, just as support for moviemaking in Jacksonville was increasing.

Mayor J.E.T. Bowden was key to support for the movie industry in Jacksonville. He saw it as the route to revitalizing the local economy, which was still recovering from the Great Fire that had devastated the city.

According to the book *History of Duval County, Florida*, page 237, by Pleasant Daniel Gold, as published by The Record Company, St. Augustine, Florida in 1928, James E.T. Bowden was "elected mayor of the town of La Villa, which was one of three municipalities which afterward formed the city of Jacksonville. In 1899 he was elected Mayor of the City of Jacksonville and held that position at the time of the great fire."

The Great Fire occurred in 1901. Between then and the start of World War I, Jacksonville was in the process of adjusting and rebuilding itself from the effects of that fire. Mayor Bowden attempted to make Jacksonville the "Winter Film Capital" and ultimate rival to Hollywood, California, as part of the projected rebirth of Jacksonville.

The book *Papers: The Jacksonville Historical Society*, a publication of the Jacksonville Historical Society. Jacksonville, Florida, 1947, provides an account of this early period of time in Jacksonville's history....

> In those days Jacksonville was doing all it could to attract other studios to the city. The Chamber of Commerce had a Motion Picture Committee appointed by President Charles H. Mann to look after the interests of the producing com-

panies and to assist in obtaining sites and equipment. On the committee were Mayor Bowden Louis R. Burnstein, W.R. Carter, George E. Leonard, Telfair Stockton and J.J. Logan.

Mayor Bowden also named a committee to help attract companies here. Members were J.B. Pound, Telfair Stockton, W.R. Carter, George Mason and H.M. Stanford. The Seaboard Air Line Railroad publicized this city's admirable climate and scenic surroundings in a further effort to appeal to the producers. The Board of County Commissioners adopted resolutions inviting film companies to locate here.

Frank Beresford, business manager of Mirror Films, urged that the city erect a municipal studio as an inducement to motion picture companies to come here, renting both studio and equipment. The present site of the Naval Air Station was suggested. Nothing came of it, however, and that was one incident that prevented Jacksonville from retaining the industry. The city did, however, extend use of the zoo in Springfield Park for housing of animals used in motion pictures.

M. Dintenfass, treasurer of the Vim Company, was one of the men engaged in motion picture production that was optimistic about Jacksonville's future, predicting that at least 100 companies would be located here by 1917. At that time Vim was spending $3,200 weekly in salaries to regulars and several hundred more dollars to 'extras.'

The Rotary Club heard leaders of the film industry at a luncheon meeting in 1916. On the program were Billy Sullivan, William A. Howell, George Grimer and Harris Gordon of Thanhouser, Arthur Albertson and Tom Boyd of Kalem, G.M. Burnstein of Vim and Paul Price, assistant director of Rolfe-Metro. When Joseph W. Engle, treasurer of the Metor Motion Picture Company, visited Jacksonville to look over the plans for a studio, he too was feted by Rotary.

Still further indications of the permanent status the film industry had attained were the opening of a school of dramatic art and motion picture acting by Pansie Cronan, former screen star from Chicago, and F.J. Seibert.

Jacksonville entertained thoughts of bringing California film companies to Jacksonville, in a bold move sending a delegation to New York City for that purpose. In the article titled *"Delegation May Be Sent to New York to Get California Motion Picture Industries"* (Florida Times-Union, January 12, 1916, section 2, page 13) it is further stated. . . .

"Mayor Bowden, Heads of Civic and Commercial Bodies and Producers Hold Conference to Formulate Plans That Will Attract Dissatisfied Element of Los Angeles Players, Who Plan to Depart from That Vicinity—Action to Be Taken at Once." The article continues by saying. . . .

Indications last night were that that officials of the city, the chamber of commerce, the tourist and convention bureau, the real estate board, the port commission, the banking interests, and the resident motion picture producers have awakened to a situation, the successful turning of which will pour at least $30,000,000 annually into local coffers and increase the resident population by over 6,000 persons. Following a conference between a committee of the producers and a similar body to be appointed by Mayor Bowden at the Hotel Mason this evening at 8 o'clock a concerted action toward a decisive end will be launched and the delegation sent northward or some other means for accomplishing this purpose determined.

The initial gun was fired at the weekly luncheon meeting of the Jacksonville Rotary club early yesterday afternoon in the Seminole hotel, when W.R. Carter announced that H.A. Kelly, superintendent of the Eagle Film and Producing Company , had informed him a few minutes before that a committee of Los Angeles producers had gone to San Francisco to confer with the chamber of commerce relative to withdrawing from the former because of restrictions thrown about the industry by the city government which have made continued activities there undesirable. He also stated that Mr. Kelly had told him that he had sent a five-hundred word telegram to the producers' committee advising them of conditions as he had found them here and inviting them to consider Florida's offerings before making a final selection.

The speaker urged upon the Rotarians the necessity of not letting escape the opportunity for securing this increasing industry by urging the civic and commercial bodies to take immediate action as well as forwarding a telegram themselves to reinforce that sent by the Eagle producer. At a final vote the matter was referred to a committee headed by Col. W. P. Corbett, which was given the authority to act.

During the afternoon President Mann of the chamber of commerce, Mayor J.E.T. Bowden, the tourist and convention bureau and the real estate board were advised of the Rotarians action and an immediate conference between officials of these organizations and the local resident producers was arranged for 5:30 o'clock at the Hotel Mason. In the meantime Mayor Bowden telegraphed the president and members of the Photoplayers Screen club of Los Angeles as follows... "As executive of Jacksonville, Fla., I extend to the moving picture fraternity of this country a cordial invitation to our city. I pledge you every consideration that is possible. You will find atmospheric conditions suitable for work necessary to carryon moving picture business. Many companies are located here now. I'm told by those connected with them static conditions are superior to any other portion of the country. Our magnificent streams, tropical foliage, in fact every condition necessary except mountain scenery obtained here. Earnestly request investigation."

Likewise General Manager H.H. Richardson of the tourist and convention bureau sent the following telegram to Mack Sennett of the Keystone Film Company in the same way. . . . "In looking for a new location you are urged to carefully investigate and consider Jacksonville, the hospitable southern city, the metropolis of Florida, a state where history is filled with the romance of the past and citizenship will give you a typical southern and sunny welcome. Our atmospheric conditions cannot be excelled. We have scenic variety of wood, forests,

Figure 1.1. Hotel Mason, Jacksonville, Florida (Blair Miller Collection).

streams and ocean beaches. We are within twenty-four hours by through trains of large Eastern cities. Our transportation facilities by rail and water excellent. Hotel accommodations ample at rates to suit all sized pocketbooks. Our people generous and open hearted. Jacksonville is the Gateway city to Florida, which is visited annually by million visitors seeking health and recreation. In fact this city has been pronounced the ideal location by many of the largest producing companies in the country.... Would suggest we send a committee to you or you to us to confer. Please pass on to interested parties."

When the conference at the Hotel Mason was called to order representatives from the Metro, Equitable, Thanhouser, Eagle, Palm and Kalem studios were present, as well as President G.A. McClellan, General Manager Richardson and Third Vice President of W.W. Smith of the tourist and convention bureau, Mayor J.E.T. Bowden, President Charles A. Brown, Jr. of the real estate board, Chairman M. Corse and A.D. Stevens of the Port commission, and J.J. Logan representing the banking interests of the city.

Mayor Bowden was unanimously elected chairman of the meeting, and a discussion immediately started toward devising a plan of action. Chairman Bowden called upon the producers for suggestions and several of them declared their pleasure at being located in Florida, each setting forth his reasons, which reflected greatly upon the climatic and scenic offerings of Los Angeles.

Director Noble of the Metro Company, which has only been here for the past week, told the committee that he found Florida without handicaps existing in California and especially about Los Angeles, where he said foggy weather almost daily made picture making impossibility for any continuous length of time. He said he had not been in this state long enough to speak authoritatively upon continuous climatic conditions but, from what had been seen during the past week, he was most favorably impressed because of the short distance between Jacksonville and New York by boat or rail and the bright light effects continuing throughout the morning and into the afternoon until shortly after 3 o'clock, which made it possible for a full day's work to be performed by the cameraman and players, without the necessity of having to cease activities during the foggy hours after 10 o'clock, which made Los Angeles unfavorable.

Other producers set forth their impressions and the whole sifted down to a sentence showed that they prefer studios in Jacksonville, because of the scenic, climatic and hospitable offerings the latter of which seems to have become a misnomer in the West. Each manifested a willingness to assist the others in inducing the dissatisfied Western companies to turn their faces toward Florida.

General Manager Richardson, of the Tourist and Convention Bureau, spoke briefly upon the local conditions in relation to the building up of a large motion picture industry. He declared this city is exactly 2,149 miles nearer New York from where all of the releases are made where is located the main offices and factories of the producers. He also cited the fact that the trip can be made south and north by steamship, which enables scenes to be made aboard, which would be important on railway trains on which the players would have to travel back and forth from New York to Los Angeles. In addition to this he said that the Atlantic seaboard cities are within twenty-four to thirty hours ride by train, which is a great time as well as money saver for the movement of large companies.

In conclusion President McClellan put through a motion that the chairman appoint a committee of three to confer with the producers this afternoon after the latter had held a conference of their own and designated a similar body to cooperate with the other in active plans for the campaign. Upon suggestion of several of the producers 4 p.m. was appointed as the hour for the joint meeting. Mayor Bowden will select his committee this morning.

When these two bodies get down to actual work this afternoon their action may result in the speedy dispatch of the delegation to New York for the purpose of conferring with the head officials of the companies with a view to turning them southward in their quest for a future home. It seemed to be the consensus of opinion at the meeting yesterday that the most effective move can be made by going to headquarters and it is for this reason that New York may be the center of attack rather than Los Angeles or San Francisco, which seems to be anxious to secure this prize itself.

George E. Leonard, president of the Rotary club and secretary of the chamber of commerce, was absent yesterday from both the luncheon and the conference in the late afternoon, owing to the fact that he is at New Orleans attending the convention of Southern Rotary Clubs. He has been one of the most active and ardent workers for the increasing of Jacksonville's coterie of motion picture producers. . . .

Should it be decided to make a counter attack upon the producers working in California, as well as the main office in New York, it is possible that he will be instructed to proceed west from New Orleans to Los Angeles to confer with the officers and members of the Photo Players Screen Club. This may be the means of communicating information to them which will prove more effective through personal contact than could possibly be obtained by letters or telegrams.

Further details are provided by a January 23, 1916 (section 1, page 4) Florida Times Union article entitled *"Louis Burstein Is to Show Film of Committeemen"*. . . .

Motion pictures of the delegation sent by Mayor Bowden to confer with the New York producers relative to landing the Los Angeles picture interests for Jacksonville will be shown at the local theaters during the next week, according to Louis Burstein, general of the Vim Film Corporation. These pictures show the delegates as they were about to board the Atlantic Coast Line New York and Florida Special train shortly after noon yesterday and again as the fast train departed with them waving a farewell from the observation platform.

"I expect to have two of these films made and have the different theaters show them the same night, each announcing the exact hour so the reel can be sent on its rounds ," said Mr. Burstein last night.

He is one of the most enthusiastic advocates of the up building of a great producing center here and the committee departed with letters of introduction from him, as well as other local producers, to the different corporation heads in the East. In addition to these the committeemen carried the 1,500 feet of film made to show views of Jacksonville to the New Yorkers.

The committee appointed by Mayor Bowden is composed of J.J. Logan, Chairman J.R. Pound, Telfair Stockton, W.R. Carter, George Mason, and H.M. Stanford.

The Florida Times Union, in an article appearing in the February 11, 1916 issue (page 10) headlines "That Genuine Welcome Is Extended to Movie Industry," noting that "Representative Business and Profession Men Bid Producers to Locate Here. Many Film Men Present State There Is No Reason Why Jacksonville Cannot Become Motion Picture Center." further details are provided in the text, as follows. . . .

> At the meeting last night of the chamber of commerce, Jacksonville, through various addresses made by its representatives in business and professional walks of life, bade producers of motion to come to Jacksonville. Enthusiasm marked all of the speeches. The great gain to payrolls and the advertising which the city will receive were some of the things emphasized.
>
> There were a number of motion picture people present, and in their addresses they stated if the newcomers get the same treatment, which has been already accorded them here, Jacksonville will soon be one of the greatest motion picture centers in the United States.
>
> J.J. Logan and Telfair Stockton, members of the local committee which visited New York with a view of inducing the companies to locate studios here, were among the speakers and they again told of the courteous manner in which they had been received there by men high in the motion picture industry. In this connection they again made mention of the fact that entrée to many people in the film industry was made possible through the courtesy of Mark M. Dintenfass, treasurer of the Vim Company.
>
> Mr. Stockton stated that Jacksonville being only twenty-seven hours away from New York was one of the biggest assets in its efforts to secure the studios. Mr. Dintenfass followed and corrected the latter's figures with reference to the amount of money sent from New York to California weekly in payrolls. Mr. Dintenfass said $2,000,000 is actually sent, instead of $1,500,000.
>
> Mayor J.E.T. Bowden declared: "I believe this is a new era in Jacksonville, not alone from a financial standpoint but the high class advertising this city will get by word of mouth of the people who work here.
>
> Louis Bernstein, of the Vim Company declares that his people are here and here to stay for at least six years longer. He made a most pleasing address and a great impression on his audience.
>
> Walter Storey stated that there is no reason why Jacksonville could not be the greatest all year-round producing city centre to the United States. W.J. Dunn, of the Eagle Company, declared that in theatrical circles the motion picture has

become the recognized contender for favor. That is why he left the stage for the camera, he said.

Riley Chamberlain, one of the well known actors of the Thanhouser interests, reminded his hearers in a genial manner that the motion picture actor is important, his face and form going on the screen long after he is dead. Following him came 'Babe' Hardy, who told some of the troubles of really being a motion picture actor.

Early in the meeting the following resolution, read by its author, John B. Callahan, councilman from the Third ward, was endorsed by the commerce board. Mr. Callahan stating that he wanted the body's endorsement of the resolution before he presents it to the council for adoption.

Be it resolved by the city council of the city of Jacksonville. That the council hereby expresses itself as being in favor of granting to motion picture companies the right to take pictures on any buildings, grounds or improvements of the city of Jacksonville, including the prison farm, waterworks and the electric light plant, upon making application to the head of the department having charge of city property.

Be it further resolved. That the board of bond trustees, the committee on public works and the board of port commissioners be requested to endorse this resolution and that they furnish to moving picture companies the right to take pictures of their respective departments.

In an article right beside the above article, also appearing in the Florida Times Union of February 11, 1916, (page 10), and a related topic is discussed. *"Moving Picture Center Plan Is Fully Discussed"* notes the following. . . .

The February meeting of the Jacksonville Chamber of Commerce held last night went on record as favoring every effort that will be made for this city becoming a great motion picture center. It was believed that a big pay roll will be the case, as well as city advertising, which will fully justify the effort being set forth at this time. Many interesting facts were set forth by the committee which went to New York in the interest of seeing producing concerns for this city. . . .

Some movie companies were enthusiastic about Jacksonville as this March 15, 1916 article, *"Motion Picture Men Hail Jacksonville as Klondike of This Growing Industry,"* portrays. It was featured in the Florida Times Union, in section 2, page 17. . . .

Joseph W. Engle, treasurer and executive head of the Metro Motion Picture Corporation was in Jacksonville from New York to look over the local field with a view of erecting a studio, was the guest of honor at a dinner in the Hotel Mason last night.

Mr. Engle's visit to Jacksonville is the direct result of the recent trip to New York of a local committee, headed by L.J. Logan during which the advantages of Jacksonville as a motion picture center were presented to the producing interests there. Mr. Engle arrived in Jacksonville Monday and after a trip about the city stated that he was most agreeably impressed with Jacksonville.

Those present at the dinner last night included members of the motion picture committee of the chamber of commerce and a few invited guests, including several other picture men who are engaged in making pictures in Jacksonville.

As he was the guest of honor, so was Mr. Engle the principal speaker, as those present were most anxious to hear what he had to say about Jacksonville after having had a more extended opportunity to see the city and its environs.

"I came here merely as an observer," said Mr. Engle, "Because I had a brief vacation coming to me. We were so impressed with the committee Jacksonville sent to New York and with the reports coming from our companies which had made pictures here that I really looked forward to my trip with a great deal of pleasure," said the speaker.

Continuing Mr. Engle said that he was wonderfully impressed with Jacksonville. "I don't mind telling you," he said, "that the statements of what you people intended to do to encourage the industry, were received with polite misgivings, as we did not think it possible in the view of other experiences in other cities." In this connection, Mr. Engle told why 'Los Angeles' had become impossible as a producing center, owing to the restrictions thrown about the business there by municipal and state authorities. He said that Jacksonville had the climate, one of the greatest assets to the business, as well as all other advantages, and spoke of Jacksonville as the possible Klondike of the picture industry. Mr. Engle spoke for over an hour, holding his hearers to the end with his able and sincere address in which he frankly stated that he was agreeably surprised over the cordial reception extended the picture men, which was free of all restrictions, such as had been placed about the industry in other places.

Mr. Engle intimated, from what he had already seen, that his company probably would come to Jacksonville in the fall. He also said that since being here he had written to personal friends at the heads of other interests, telling them what Jacksonville offered.

Among the other speakers was William Steiner, of the serial interests, now here making a thirty-two reel picture, entitled the Yellow Peril. Mr. Steiner called South Jacksonville the Jersey of the north side of the river. He said that Los Angeles has nothing that Jacksonville can not get, and spoke of the Florida metropolis as the only city in the world, where you can get anything you want, with reference, of course to the movie business. The speaker said that his company would probably make several other big serials after it had finished the Yellow Peril.

Louis Bernstein, of the Vim Co., who has apparently become a fixture in Jacksonville, was another enthusiastic speaker in lauding the advantages of the city.

J.J. Logan, chairman of the motion picture committee, presided, and among those present, besides the speakers already mentioned, were Thomas P. Denham, J.J. Heard, A.F. Perry, W.B. McQuade, John D. Baker, George E. Leonard,

Thomas W. Haney, F.C. Roach, J.E.T. Bowden, W.A. Elliott, A.E. Lamberton, E.E. Cohen, W.R. Carter, Telfair Stockton, as well as others.

Many of the guests were also called upon for short addresses, all of whom spoke in encouraging tones , and all pledging themselves to work for the best interests of Jacksonville in the movie game.

The Florida Times-Union of March 17, 1916 (section 2, page 13) concerns plans for a movie ball in Jacksonville. The article is titled *"Great Movie Ball Planned for Benefit of Two Charities,"* with a sub headline that reads *"Thanhouser Club Making Elaborate Plans for Brilliant Affair in Windsor Hotel Night of March 31—Children's Home Society of Florida and Actor's Fund Will Be Beneficiaries".* . . .

> The actor's charity ball to be held at the Windsor Hotel on the night of March 31 will be one of the most elaborate affairs of its kind ever held in this city, according to more recent announcement from the committee in charge of the arrangements. The proceeds are to be divided between the Actors Fund of America and the Children's Home Society.
>
> The Thanhouser club is the organization under the auspices of which the ball is to be given in response to an appeal sent out by the Actors Fund of America, which is endeavoring to raise the sum of $500,000 in fifteen weeks. The call has been on the motion picture interests to provide for its share and the ball is to be the means of Jacksonville's actors contributing. Mayor Bowden has designated the Children's Home Society as the organization to receive the other half of the proceeds.
>
> Manager Kavanaugh, of the Windsor hotel, has donated the use of the mammoth ball room for the occasion and other local people are also assisting the committee in preparing for a successful evening. Tickets are on sale at Furchgott's, The Big Store, Levy's, Aragon hotel, Hotel Mason, Seminole hotel and all picture studios.
>
> The appeal sent out by the Actor's Fund of America is as follows. . . .
>
> "Everyone in the film business is requested to help the motion campaign for the Actor's Fund of America. Raise $500,000 in fifteen weeks. We appeal to all actors and actresses in the motion picture industry. The executive committee requests every actor and actress to contribute some money to the motion picture campaign for the Actor's Fund of America—an optional sum—whatever you can afford."
>
> Before the war the calls for help from artists in distress in different parts of the United States amounted to $1,000 a year, and now about $70,000 a year is disbursed among the needy in the artistic field. To give first and ask explanations afterward is the slogan of the distinguished president, Mr. Daniel Frohman. Let us all be as charitable as our purse will allow. The motion picture campaign expects to contribute $500,000 in fifteen weeks, and we need your help to raise this amount.

Figure 1.2. Windsor Hotel, Jacksonville, Florida (Florida State Archives).

Figure 1.3. Windsor Hotel, Jacksonville, Florida (Florida State Archives).

Figure 1.4. Windsor Hotel, Jacksonville, Florida (Florida State Archives).

After having pleased the difficult public in the springtime of their lives, those who are going down the other side of the hill broken, helpless and alone—need your help! Look into your own hearts and you cannot resist the call for help. What greater obligation and what greater pleasure can there be than to sustain those whose misfortune tugs at your heart strings? With the million dollars necessary to endow this fund and the Actors Home on Staten Island annual collections are needed.

The officers of the Thanhouser club are: President, George A. Grimmer; vice presidents, Mayor Bowden and George Webber; secretary, W. Ray Johnston; treasurer, Leo Wirth; chairman of the entertainment committee, Harris Gordon. Members if the entertainment committee are: Thomas Curran, Boyd Marshall, George Welch, Walter Hires, William Burt, Sully Guard, Morgan Jones, William McNulty, Charles Owens, Arthur Bauer, Benjamin Ross, James Murray, William Alexander, Lawrence Williams, Bert Bowman. The patrons will include Mayor Bowden, W. Eugene Moore, Ernest Warde, W.A. Howell and George Foster Platt.

An article in the Florida Metropolis newspaper (May 14, 1916, page 5D) echoes the sense of confidence people felt about the future of the movie industry in Jacksonville. Entitled *"Jax to Offer Inducements to Movie Producers,"* proclaimed "September First Will See Wholesale Exodus From New York to This City by Motion Picture Companies—Local Producers Confident of Move This Way"....

Jacksonville will offer many inducements to the producer of motion pictures to come to this city this fall and settle permanently, but these inducements will not be in any way 'financial' or rather that is the way it looks now. They will be principally 'the good will of our people.' The hearty co-operation of our municipal government, the right hand of fellowship by the Jacksonville Chamber of Commerce and the 'unexcelled atmosphere' of our hotels.

The motion picture producer of importance does not need 'financial' aid, such as could be given him here, all he needs is what has been said above, and with this and 'to be let alone' he will make 'movies' and prosper, and the citizens of this city from the richest to the poorest will prosper with him.

In speaking of the inducements offered the producers, the first includes the idea that citizens of this city "must not look on the motion picture player as an alien," but as an artist and one of us. We have had several hundred film artists in our midst since last November, and although many people looked askance at them at first, they soon won their way to our hearts and this confidence has none of them violated.

The second inducement means the help of our mayor and city officials. Laws have to be passed benefiting the producer in this city, and also protecting him, and every motion picture director or player who has visited this city has become a 'booster.'

The third inducement is the help of the principal civic organization, the Jacksonville Chamber of Commerce, with its some 2,200 live members. Whenever 'locations' are wanted this body will gladly find them, and their fees are only the 'good will' of the producer. Its secretary, George E. Leonard, has been one of the most active citizens of this city in inducing the movies to locate here, and it is all through the Chamber of Commerce that several of the studios we have now were secured.

The fourth, last but not least inducement is that of our hostelries. The movie player is like other artists, he likes to gather at some favorite spot and mingle with fellow members in the profession, and there must be some kind of amusement provided for him, other than that which he can and will make. Jacksonville's finest hotels excel in furnishing amusement for the pleasure lovers, and most any night one may stroll to the Mason and find his or her friend listening to the strains of perfect music in the beautiful Japanese roof garden or to the Seminole, where the light fantastic is being indulged in the handsome marble dining room or in the Windsor, where the music of falling waters mingle with that of a superb orchestra.

These are not the only pleasure producing spots, however. There are the several clubs in and around the city, and the beautiful Atlantic Beach Hotel, at Atlantic Beach, where thousands annually seek the cool waters of the briny deep, and enjoy the pleasures of pulling their favorite member of the piscatorial tribe from its placid depths.

These are the inducements offered the player, producer, owner and camera man, the later who is one of the most insistent that conditions be perfect from all sides and angles. We offer Mr. Cameraman the best climate in the world conducive to the filming of motion pictures. Hours unlimited and atmosphere better than the best. Any cameraman who has ever filmed a picture in this city will verify this, and we quote from such authorities as Jim Carleton, Lawrence Williams, Billy Sullivan, Jack Collins, Al Moses, George K. Hollister and Harry Keepers.

Take it all in all, where is there an Arcadia other than Jacksonville in the movie We are twenty-four hours from Broadway—think of it—only twenty-four hours from the center of the world, where, when it is 20 below zero we are dipping daily in the beautiful ocean.

An article in the November 3, 1916 issue of the Florida Times-Union (page 9, section 2) carried the headline *"Screen Club to be Perfected at Meeting November 16"* with the following words. . . .

Steps toward organization of the Screen Club of Jacksonville were taken at a meeting held in the Hotel Mason last night, where W.R. Carter was elected temporary chairman and several committees appointed to report on organization and nominations at the next meeting called for November 16. The meeting was attended by forty-nine people, who responded to the call sent out several days ago by D. Joyce Milbery.

The club is to have upon its membership all those connected or interested in the motion picture industry including both active workers in the studios, members of the press, film exchange men, and motion picture theater operators. It will be a social and cooperative organization.

Among the well known men who delivered short talks upon the needs of such an organization were Mayor Bowden, George Mason, Louis Burstein, Harry Meyers, and W.R. Carter.

The committees appointed and instructed to report at the next meeting were:

Organization Committee: Storm V. Boyd, Louis Burstein and Ferdinand Perez.

Nominations Committee: H.T. Tucker, Mr. Barton, Harry Meyers, D. Joyce Milbery and E.D. Jall.

Headquarters Committee: George H. Mason, Mayor Bowden and Babe Hardy.

Change was constant in the early film industry. Companies divided, merged, regrouped and renamed on a regular basis, as you will see in the following chapters.

The reader must be aware that the fast moving, mercurial nature of the business sometimes causes historical confusion. . . .

Chapter Two

Kalem Company, Inc

The Kalem Company, Inc. was originally started by George Kleine, Samuel Long (sales manager) and Frank K. Marion (journalist) with combined assets of $600. Kalem Company was located on Tallyrand Avenue. An alternate address was given as 1959 Pleasant View, in Fairfield, a suburb of Jacksonville.

The name Kalem was formed from their initials, K_L_M. In 1909 Kalem's administrative offices were located in New York City at 131 West 24th Street—but by 1915 had moved to the Eastman Kodak Building at 235-239 West 23rd Street in New York City.

Sidney Olcott was in charge of the production company that located in Jacksonville, where Kalem produced the Sis Hopkins comedy series and an Ivy Close comedy series. Bob Ellis was the director of the Sis Hopkins comedies. T.J. Dow was the manager of moving pictures.

An October 20, 1913 article, in the *Florida Times Union*, has much to say about the expanding Kalem presence in Jacksonville. In the article titled *"Kalem Company Arrives for the Winter Season"* it is learned that the company is "the largest that has yet to be sent." Furthermore, the Kalem Company, one of the leading firms engaged in the manufacture and production of motion pictures in the United States and which has had companies in Jacksonville for the past two winter seasons, will use this city as a field of operations again this winter and a company composed of sixteen talented motion picture artists has arrived in the city preparatory to taking a series of pictures in this locality.

> The company is practically the same as the one which held forth in Jacksonville during the past spring and winter, with the exception that it is much larger, the management of the company realizing the great advantages that exist in this vicinity, owing to remarkably favorable climatic conditions, as well as wonder-

ful scenic advantages, every scenario necessary for the production of motion pictures being naturally provided, with the possible exception of those requiring a mountainous background....The company will be greatly strengthened during the winter months by the addition of a number of other artists, who will be sent here from other stations. . . .

An October 20, 1913 article, in the *Florida Times Union*, has much to say about the expanding Kalem presence in Jacksonville. In the article titled *"Kalem Company Arrives for the Winter Season"* it is learned that the company is "the largest that has yet to be sent." Furthermore, the Kalem Company, one of the leading firms engaged in the manufacture and production of motion pictures in the United States and which has had companies in Jacksonville for the past two winter seasons, will use this city as a field of operations again this winter and a company composed of sixteen talented motion picture artists has arrived in the city preparatory to taking a series of pictures in this locality.

The company is practically the same as the one which held forth in Jacksonville during the past spring and winter, with the exception that it is much larger, the management of the company realizing the great advantages that exist in this vicinity, owing to remarkably favorable climatic conditions, as well as wonderful scenic advantages, every scenario necessary for the production of motion pictures being naturally provided, with the possible exception of those requiring a mountainous background....The company will be greatly strengthened during the winter months by the addition of a number of other artists, who will be sent here from other stations. . . .

The popularity of the Sis Hopkins, and Rose Melville, was indisputable. The *Moving Picture World* of December 25, 1915 (page 2338) described the phenomenon. . . .

No other character creation of the stage has ever taken so complete a hold on a player's identity as that of Sis Hopkins. Though well known as a dramatic actress and a musical comedy favorite before the character of Sis Hopkins leaped into country-wide fame that unique character became so popular that Rose Melville has never since been allowed to be anything but Sis Hopkins. Without the possibilities for universal popularity presented by the screen the Sis Hopkins character took the country by storm a decade ago, and the pig-tailed hair and gingham-aproned girl of the farm reached the heights of becoming a fad. Sis Hopkins dolls, Sis Hopkins aprons, and Sis Hopkins hair-ribbons were among the many crazes of the time. She is the only player known to have a national publication named after her, when the quaintly humorous sayings of the character inspired the establishment the "Sis Hopkins Library of Fun," published by Leslie-Judge Company.

Rose Melville was interviewed in 1916, for a book about the comedy filmmaking personalities called *Film Flashes: The Wit and Wisdom of a Nation in Pictures*. She had the following to say about her career. . . .

"I've tried other plays, but the public wanted Sis Hopkins, and so I gave them Sis Hopkins for eleven years," says Rose Melville, "and here comes Sis in the pictures, at last. And I have found out why so many stage stars have jumped at chances to go into the pictures. They may talk about art and a new field all they like. Don't let 'em fool you, my dear. The screen is the greatest weight reducer ever invented for players who are threatened with—well, let us call it, delicately, embonpoint. Look at me—look at me. Do you get my meaning?"

Miss Melville swirled energetically to her feet and danced lightly about on one toe. Her lines were considerably linier than they had been. For, deny it as you may, Sis Hopkins had begun to get just a wee bit—just a trifle—stoutish of late years.

"I've lost ten pounds. Congratulate me," she said with the captivating Sis Hopkins smile and that luring Sis Hopkins voice. "When they named them 'moving pictures, they were right 'Moving' is the word, for I haven't had a chance to stand still for sixty successive second since the camera began to grind at me."

"Be thankful you were Sis Hopkins and not Helen Hazards," it was suggested.

"Right now let me tell you that 'Hazards of Helen' girl hasn't anything on me in the way of bruised muscles and sore spots," said Sis. "First I hit my nose a whack and went around here feeling as important as you please with my swelled-up nose, and then I cut my lip; and as for the number of times I have whacked my poor head crawling around under tables and running against furniture, I never could tell you. Shucks! I am qualifying right now to enter athletic competition, with obstacle races my specialty, if I ever get out of this alive. Talk about Muldoon's sanitarium! If some of these liverish chaps would go into motion pictures, they'd soon get the grouch shaken out of their system."

"My first experience frightened me to death. I'll face an audience and make fun for them, because I know they have paid their good money to watch me; but to step out of the studio, gowned in full Sis Hopkins regalia, and walk across a Jacksonville street before a gaping crowd of spectators, made me feel as if I was an entire circus—Greatest Show on Earth."

"Are you doing some new Sis Hopkins stunts?"

"Some new Sis Hopkins stunts? My dear, that's what is reducing me—doing these new stunts. In my play I did the same things every performance, but in these pictures I can manufacture new business all the time. It's great! I can do all the tomboy tricks I wanted to do when I was a little girl."

Rose Melville wrote a humorous account of her first days at Kalem for The Moving Picture World January 1916 (page 585) issue. . . .

"When they named them moving pictures they were right," says Rose Melville, creator of Sis Hopkins. "The accent is strongly on the 'move,' for I haven't been stationary for sixty successive seconds since the camera was first set up. Now, I know why so many stage stars have jumped at opportunities to take up motion picture work. The screen is the greatest weight-reducer ever invented for players threatened by an excess of embonpoint. I feel sure that I have lost ten pounds already."

It is in a letter to the Kalem Company officials received last week that Sis Hopkins gives her views of motion picture work following her first week in the studio at Jacksonville. As a candid expression of the emotions of a stage player making her first bow to the camera the communication is of unusual interest.

"Well, the first week and the first picture are over," the letter reads. "And right now, let me tell you that your 'Hazards of Helen' girl cannot show me anything new in the way of bruises and sore muscles. I knocked my nose against something—was too busy to find out just what it was—and have a bruised lip and am sore all over from crawling from one room into another and running at fast speed around tables. After I get through with pictures I plan to take up athletic competition with obstacle racing as my specialty."

"The first day outdoor found me more thoroughly frightened than I was on the night I first stepped out of the wings to face a Broadway audience. Just think of walking across the main thoroughfare of the thriving city of Jacksonville in full regalia and before a large crowd. I can assure you I felt like the 'Greatest Show on Earth.'"

"But with it all—and without the ten pounds—I must say that I am beginning to like the work. If the picture audiences get as many laughs out of my actions on the screen as I do in the comparative quiet of my dressing room, we are going to get along together like old friends. I know I am enjoying the work for I am really anxious for the next picture to start. The screen offers such unlimited scope for your efforts to please that it makes the stage feel like a Punch and Judy show in comparison. In conclusion, I want to express my appreciation of the surroundings here. Everyone has been most kind and we have a real happy family here at the studio."

Kalem brought Ivy Close to America from England in 1916. She was an English stage star prior to making the Ivy Close comedies in Jacksonville. In a May 20.1916 article in Moving Picture World Kalem Vice President William Wright had the following to say about her filmmaking. . . .

While no definite announcement has been made as to Kalem's plans for presenting the famous beauty on the screen Mr. Wright, of Kalem, was emphatic in his declaration last week that she would be featured in one-reel subjects. "Since our practice of putting our strongest efforts into the short subjects is well known," he declared, "It may be expected that Miss Close will be seen in the short lengths. We made an innovation in presenting such a high salaried star as Rose Melville in single-reel Sis Hopkins comedies, but the overwhelming success of the plan makes it certain that the large figures of Miss Close's contract will not cause us to abandon our loyalty to the short subject."

Kalem studios were located in Santa Monica, California, near Mack Sennett's Keystone studios, and on Tallyrand Avenue in Jacksonville. The Jacksonville studio grounds included the Roseland Hotel and another house on Tallyrand Avenue. It was a plantation house where Kalem established Jacksonville's first twelve month studio.[1] Tallyrand Avenue would later become Clarkson Street. Kalem's President Frank Marion bought and lived in a house on Riverside Avenue.[2]

The Roseland Hotel was leased by Kalem. It was "a small but fully equipped boarding hotel which occupied a whole block of riverfront, three acres of lawn and had its own bowling alley, tennis courts and croquet grounds."[3]

Further details are provided in an advertisement /article that appeared in the March 5, 1905 issue of the Florida Times Union newspaper. On page 22 the Roseland Hotel is described in the headline as "ideal location on beautiful St. Johns River" in a "select resident section, a high class tourist and family hotel." The article's text provides further details. . . . "Whole block river front, three acre lawn. Bowling alley, tennis and croquet grounds. Golf links two blocks away .Good boating and fishing from private pier 1,000 feet long. Unexcelled cuisine. Northern cooking. Persons seeking a delightful winter home are invited to inspect the superior accommodations offered. . . . Special rates $8, $10, and $12 weekly; $1.50 and $2.00 per day. American plan. Illustrated booklet mailed." The article was written by Roseland proprietor, E.K. Ekholm.

Kalem originally came to Jacksonville in 1907, where they filmed part of their five reel feature film *From the Manger to the Cross*. That completed, the company went to the Holy Land to film the remainder of the film—not returning to Jacksonville until 1912.[4]

In 1913 Sidney Olcott decided that Kalem should make feature films that were five reels long, instead of the three reel length that they'd traditionally used. When upper level management refused to consider this idea, Olcott left to start his own feature film company.

Midway through 1914, Kalem outgrew Roseland—and added an outdoor stage capable of allowing three separate films to be filmed at the same time and a glass roofed indoor studio (with a 54 by 60 foot stage and a $20,000 lighting system). When complete, they were able to plan filming twelve months in advance.[5]

Kalem founder Samuel Long died in 1915. By 1916 Kalem was filming full time (year round) in Florida. The company filmed two Sis Hopkins comedies per week in Jacksonville. Rose Melville's Kalem film debut, as Sis Hopkins, was Friday March 3, 1918, in the comedy *A Leap Year Wooing*. The comedy *A Flock of Skeletons* was to have been her first film, but it was damaged while being developed—necessitating the refilming of some of the scenes.

Figure 2.1. Roseland Hotel (Florida State Archives).

Figure 2.2. Roseland Hotel (Florida State Archives). Picture of the hotel and surrounding area where the Kalem Company came in the winter of 1908, pioneering the movie industry in Jacksonville.

(Yet Rose Melville was no stranger to the part of Sis Hopkins. Beginning in 1889 she had played Sis Hopkins on the vaudeville stage. She repeated her role, yet again; in September 1899 play version of *Sis Hopkins*, which played in Buffalo, New York.)

Some other cast members of the Sis Hopkins comedies were: Henry Murdock, Frank Minzey, Mary Kennedy, Richard Purdon, Olive West, Arthur Albertson and Robert Ellis.

Lloyd Hamilton and Bud Duncan were starred in a series of "Ham and Bud" comedies under the Kalem banner. *The Moving Picture World* trade magazine, in the March 10th, 1917 issue, described their comedy antics. . . .

> Those funny fellers—Ham and Bud, in everyday life Lloyd V. Hamilton and A.E. Duncan—have been induced to affix their signatures to long-term contracts insuring their continued appearance in the "Ham" comedies released by Kalem.
>
> Their action sets at rest a number of rumors that this famous comedy pair were about to sever their pleasant relations of over two years duration with the Kalem Company. While it is a fact that several companies were anxious to secure their services, both Ham and Bud declare that they never contemplated a change; that they would in fact feel sadly out of place under any other banner.

Figure 2.3. Comedian Team of Ham and Bud (Kalem) (Florida State Archives). Credit: Wisconsin Center for Film and Theater Research.

Judging from the volume of letters received by the Kalem Company from exhibitors who have voluntarily praised the "Ham" comedies, this bit of news will prove most interesting to the trade at large.

There recently appeared in a popular magazine an article discussing the psychology of comedy pictures. The author of that article paid Ham one of the sincerest compliments he has ever received when he said: "No one has ever questioned the mirth-provoking ability of Ham {Lloyd V. Hamilton} ably seconded by diminutive "Bud" Duncan. I do not know of a single comedian, past or present, stage or screen, whose very appearance is more inductive to a hearty guffaw than this same Ham whose comedies bear his abbreviated name. He is, beyond a doubt, the most talented of all the screen people and you realize it more with each succeeding picture.

Treating his subject from another angle this author went on to say that Ham need never resort to slapstick methods because with his knowledge of pantomime and make-up it was totally unnecessary. As a matter of fact there is a time and place for slapstick business but it is used sparingly in the "Ham" comedies, which are unusually clean and free from vulgarity and therefore popular in all communities.

The Kalem organization also announces the acquisition of Al Santell as a director for its "Ham" comedies. His very first picture, *Efficiency Experts?* is a riot of fun. The action centers around a marvelously efficient lawn mower that can be turned loose on any lawn and shear to perfection. His second production is titled *Bulls or Bullets?* and deals with the trial and tribulations of Ham and Bud in the impersonation of a famous bull fighter and his faithful matador.

Kalem regards its prompt action in retaining the services of these premier comedians and the selection of Mr. Santell to direct them as acts directly calculated to benefit the exhibitors of the entire country. "We're making the best comedies in the field today, bar none," said a representative of the Kalem Company when giving out the information about re-signing Ham and Bud.

In the book Clown Princes and Court Jesters, by Kalton C. Lahue and Samuel Gill, Ham and Bud Comedies are described in a chapter which begins on page 170. . . .

Ham and Bud began working together in their own comedies in mid-1914, but the 'Ham and Bud' series began officially with Ham at the Garbageman's Ball in March 1915. Both comedians dressed in the ill-fitting clothes regarded at the time as standard comic garb, but over 6 feet tall and weighing more than 200 pounds, Hamilton appeared colossal in comparison to little (4 ft.,11 inch) Bud Duncan. This great contrast in size played a very prominent part in their Kalem comedies. . . .

During 1916-17, the team's popularity suffered because the Kalem product was being handled by the General Film Company, the distribution arm of the Patent Trust. General Film had lost considerable ground before the determined onslaught of independent firms and public exposure to Ham and Bud lessened each month as fewer exhibitors dealt with General Film. Their association with Kalem came to an end just before Frank Marion sold out to Vitagraph in 1917.

However the popularity of Kalem's one-reel comedies declined when World War I started. Concurrently Kalem's most popular players were being signed by other companies—sometimes even earning higher salaries.

Kalem tried unsuccessfully to consolidate all of its studio resources in California, by closing the Jacksonville facility in 1917. However, within a year they had gone completely out of business.

The November 23, 1918 issue (page 848) of The Moving Picture trade magazine included an article entitled "Goldwyn Buys 'Sis Hopkins' As Vehicle for Miss Normandy. The article explained. . . .

> The next picture which Mabel Normand will make for Goldwyn will be a screen version of 'Sis Hopkins.' Goldwyn acquired the rights to this famous Hoosier play from Rose Melville, who wrote and created and played the part for nearly a quarter of a century. No play on the American stage has a more curious history than 'Sis Hopkins.
>
> To the present generation of New York theatergoers it is known only by hearsay . . . In fact 'Sis Hopkins' is of its kind a classic. Four people have made fortunes out of it and retired. Rose Melville and her husband, Frank Minzey, toured America with it year after year for nearly twenty-five years, always making the same sure profit, and usually playing to about the same audiences. In both large and small towns all over the country many people would go to see Rose Melville in 'Sis Hopkins" regularly once a year. Out of the proceeds the Minzeys have left the stage, and acquired a large estate on the shores of Lake George.
>
> 'Sis Hopkins' began as a specialty, which Miss Melville did in between the acts of 'Zeb,' when playing with the Baldwin-Melville stock company in the early nineties. Born and brought up in Indiana, she had made quite a study of Hoosier types. Her amusing caricature of the gawky farmer's daughter made such an effect that she was engaged to do it in 'Little Christopher' at the Garden Theater in 1894 and subsequently in 'The Prodigal Father' and 'By the Sad Sea Waves.' Later on Miss Melville went into vaudeville with 'Sis,' and was so successful there that she was persuaded to elaborate the sketch into a three-act play.
>
> The characterization and the dialogue were entirely Miss Melville's. As a matter of fact, 'Sis' is one of those parts that grew rather than being written, because Miss Melville never ceased building and elaborating the part. It will be an ideal character for Mabel Normand in pictures. The character and situations offer ideal opportunities for her to build comic sense on.

KALEM FILMOGRAPHY

One Sis Hopkins's comedy *She Came, She Saw, She Conquered* featured Rose Melville, Ed Lawrence, Minerva Florence, Frank Minsey, Arthur

Figure 2.4. Mabel Normand in the film Sis Hopkins (Moving Picture World 2/8/1919).

Albertson, Marjorie Cohan, Henry Murdock and Richard Purdon (*Sunday Metropolis*, 3/1/16, p. 5)

The Sis Hopkins comedy *When Things Go Wrong* cast included Arthur Albertson, Mary Kennedy, Olive West, Richard Purdon, Henry Murdock and Frank Minsey. It was released Friday, March 24, 1918 (*Sunday Metropolis*, 3/19/18, p. 5).

HAM AND BUD COMEDIES

1914. *Ham the Piano Mover* (November), *The Peach at the Ball* (November), *Ham the Iceman* (November), *Bud, Bill and the Waiter* (December), *The Winning Whiskers* (December), *Love, Oil and Grease* (December).

1915. *Ham and the Sausage Factory* (February), *Ham and the Jitney Bus* (February), *Ham at the Garbage Gentleman's Ball* (March),*Ham Among the Redskins* (March), *Ham in the Harem* (March), *Ham's Harrowing Duel* (April), *Ham's Easy Eats* (May), *Ham the Detective* (May),*Ham in the Nut Factory* (June), *Ham at the Fair* (June), *In High Society* (June), *The Merry Moving Men* (June), *Some Romance* (July), *A Flashlight Flivver* (July), *The Spook Raisers* (July), *Ham the Statue* (or *The Toilers*)(July), *The Hypnotic Monkey* (August), *The Winning Wash* (August), *Ham and the Experiment* (August*), Ham at the Beach* (August).

1916. *Ham Takes a Chance* (February), *Ham the Diver* (February), *Winning the Widow* (February), *Maybe Moonshine* (March), *Ham Agrees with Sherman* (March), *Ham and the Hermit's Daughter* (March), *Millionaires by Mistake* (April), *Ham and Preparedness* (April), *Ham's Waterloo* (April), *Ham and the Masked Marvel* (April), *The Tank Town Troupe* (April),*Ham's Busy Day* (May), *Seaside Romeos* (June), *The Alaskan Mouse Hound* (June), *The Beggar and His Child* (June), *Ham the Explorer* (June), *Midnight at the Old Mill* (June),*The Peach Pickers* (July), *The Baggage Smashers* (July), *The Great Detective* (July),*Ham's Whirlwind Finish* (July), *The Heart Menders* (August), *Good Evening, Judge!* (August), *Ham's Strategy* (August),*The Star Boarders* (August), *Ham in the Drug Store* (August), *Ham the Fortune Teller* (September), *Patented by Ham* (September), *The Mud Cure* (September), *Bumping the Bumps* (September*), One Step Too Far* (October), *The Love Magnet* (October), *The Sauerkraut Symphony* (October), *The Bogus Booking Agents* (October), *The Merry Motor Menders* (October), *A Desperate Duel* (November), *The New Salesman* (November), *Rival Fakers* (November), *Dudes for a Day* (November), *The Jailbirds* (December), *The Iceman and the Artist* (December).

1917. Rival Romeos (January), Cupid's Caddies (January), The Blundering Blacksmiths (January), Ghost Hounds (February), The Model Janitor

(February), A Flyer in Flap-jacks (February), Efficiency Experts (February), Bulls or Bullets (March), The Bogus Bride (March), A Misfit Millionaire (April), The Deadly Doughnut (April), Doubles and Troubles (April), Bandit, Beware! (April), Hard Times in Hard Scrabble (April), A Menagerie Mixup (May), The Hobo Raid (May), A Day Out of Jail (June), The Boot and the Loot (October), Politics in Pumpkin Center (October), Whirlwind of Whiskers (October), The Onion Magnate's Revenge (October).

NOTES

1. According to the article "Hooray for Jacksonville," as appeared in the *Port of Jacksonville* magazine of December/January 1985.
2. J.C. Craig article in Florida Times Union.
3. Richard Alan Nelson, in *Lights! Camera ! Florida!*, page 17.
4. C.H. Harris letter 11/4/78.
5. From Lights! Camera! Florida!, starting on page 13.

Chapter Three

Lubin Motion Picture Company

Siegmund Lubin, upon hearing of Kalem's success in Jacksonville, personally came to Jacksonville to select a location for a Lubin studio. He found that location, at 740-750 Riverside Avenue, between Roselle Street and Edison Avenue, at a building that had been the temporary home of the Florida Yacht Club.

The club, originally on Market Street, had their clubhouse burned down on May 3, 1901. So they had moved to the Riverside Avenue site, only to move again (November of 1907) to a facility at the intersection of St. John's Avenue and Willowbranch Avenue. This third move left Riverside Avenue free for Lubin to rent, to the Vim Company, in 1916. Lubin and Vim were both allied with Edison's Patent Trust and distributed by the affiliated General Film Company.

The studio encompassed a space 50 feet by 450 feet, which extended from Riverside Avenue to the bank of the St. John River. In addition an exterior 52 foot by 125 foot stage was also built.

A firsthand account of the studio was provided by the October 8, 1912 issue of The Florida Times Union newspaper.[1]

> The popular Lubin Motion Picture Company, which spent the past winter in Jacksonville and made a number of most interesting photo plays in this city, will return shortly and will take a series of motion picture plays in this immediate vicinity that will even surpass those of the past season....
>
> Among the most interesting pictures that were obtained by the Lubin Company last week was one entitled Hans and Fritz in Jacksonville, Florida, which contained some of the best views of the Florida metropolis and which was commented on with favor throughout the nation.

This picture was taken by the company with the cooperation of the Jacksonville Board of Trade and among other interesting features showed the efficiency and strength of the local fire and police departments. . . .

At all events the Lubin Company will receive a cordial welcome and the lovers of motion pictures hope that the company will be as successful during the coming season as it has been in the past.

The company has leased the property formerly owned by the Florida Yacht club, situated on Riverside Avenue, between Date and Roselle streets.

Oliver "Babe" Hardy started his film career at the Lubin Jacksonville studio in 1914, and remained with Lubin until August of 1915. He did briefly leave the studio (after the 1914-1915 winter filming season) to work in the New York City area—returning to Jacksonville in the spring of 1915. Hardy's first film with Lubin was *Outwitting Dad*, which was released April 21, 1914.

The Lubin comedy unit, under the direction of Arthur D. Hotaling, had originally only spent winters at the Lubin's Jacksonville studio. They would go to Lubin's Philadelphia studio in April, spend the months of May and June in Atlantic City, move on to Maine and Canada until fall, then return to Jacksonville. Their comedies were made in split reels—about 500 feet long or five minutes in length. Another 500 foot film, of a completely different subject, was also included in that reel. This was a technique also used by Mack Sennett and the Keystone Film Company in California, as well as other companies.

What was perhaps Lubin's earliest Jacksonville film, with comic elements, was made in 1912. It was also, as such, an advertisement for Jacksonville. The *Florida Times-Union*, of March 21, 1912[2] noted that it would. . . .

Probably be entitled *A Busy Day in Jacksonville, Florida*. The film will be in the nature of a view of the city, though there will be enough comedy interjected to make it thoroughly entertaining.

The picture will contain views of the most attractive sections of Jacksonville with enough comedy interjected to make motion picture theaters throughout the country. The picture will be an excellent advertisement for the city, and will doubtless attract great attention in every city in which it is shown.

Secretary H.H. Richardson, of the Jacksonville Board of Trade is interested in the picture owing to the great benefit that will be derived by the city from its exhibition, and is assisting the Lubin Company in every way possible.

An effort will be made to induce the local battalion of the National Guard of Florida to give a parade tomorrow afternoon which, if given, will be a part of the picture. It is hoped by the board of trade that the officers of the local military will see their way clear to lend the use of the troops for the occasion.

Yesterday afternoon views were taken of the fire department, and interesting pictures were taken of the apparatus in motion. Views of Main Street were also taken from the top of street cars.

The picture is as yet far from complete, and a number of interesting views of the busiest and most attractive portions of the city will be taken in a few days.

Secretary Richardson stated last night that in his opinion the picture would be of untold value to Jacksonville from an advertising standpoint.

Lubin closed its Jacksonville studio on February 13, 1915. By November of that year the studio had been leased to the Vim Comedy Company. At this same time Oliver Hardy, returning from the New York City area, after off season stints working in films for Casino, Novelty, Star Light, Edison, Pathe and the Wharton Bros. Inc. "Get-Rich-Quick Wallingford" series, joined the Vim Comedy Company. (Babe had also worked in the New York City area following Lubin's 1914-1915 winter season—not returning to Jacksonville and Lubin until the spring of 1915.)[3] Vitagraph bought all of the assets that Lubin owned—then united itself, Lubin, Selig and Essanay to become V-L-S-E.

LUBIN COMEDIES FILMOGRAPHY

With Oliver Norvell "Babe" Hardy. All are split-reel comedies unless otherwise noted. The second half of the split-reel is noted in parenthesis, with the month of release. Where the film was issued in England with a different second half film that is also noted.

1914. *Outwitting Dad* (April, with *The Rube's Duck*), *Casey's Birthday* (May, with A *Blind Business*), *Building a Fire* (May, with *The Burglar's Help*), *He Won a Ranch* (May, with *Her Horrid Honeymoon*), *For Two Pins* (May, with *The Particular Cowboys*), *A Tango Tragedy* (May, with a cartoon called *Circus Time in Toyland*), *A Brewery Town Romance* (June, with *Summer Love*. In England, *Circus Toys in Toyland* replaced *Summer Love*), *A Female Cop* (June, with Fire! Fire!), *Good Cider* (June, with a documentary called *The Shell Comb Industry), Long May It Wave* (June, with *Getting Solid with Pa*), *His Sudden Recovery* (June, with *Who's Boss?* In England *The Shell Comb Industry* replaced *Who's Boss?*), *The Kidnapped Bride* (July, with *It's a Shame*), *Worms will Turn* (July, with *Temper and Temperament*), *The Rise of the Johnsons* (August, with *She Gave Him a Rose*), *He Wanted Work* (August, with *The Cook Next Door*), *They Bought a Boat* (August, with *The Puncture Proof Sock Man*. In England, *The Cook Next Door* replaced *The Puncture Proof Sock Man), Back to the Farm* (August), *Making Auntie Welcome* (August, with *Sometimes It Works*), *The Green Alarm* (September, with *Never Too Old), A Fool There Was* (September), Pins *Are Lucky* (September, with *The German Band), Jealous James* (September, with *Jinx the Barber*), *When the Ham Turned* (October), *The Smuggler's Daughter* (October. In

England the comedy was called *Love and Limberger*), *She Married for Love* (October, with *Love and Title)*, *The Soubrette and the Simp* (October, with a cartoon called *The Interrupted Nap*), *The Honor of the Force* (November, with *Kidnapping the Kid*. In England *Brown's Cook* was substituted for *Kidnapping the Kid*), *The Daddy of Them All* (November, with *The Tale of a Coat*), *She Was the Other* (November, with *Cheap Transportation*. In England *the Bomb* was substituted), *The Daddy of Them All* (November, with *The Tale of the Coat*), *Mother's Baby Boy* (November, with *He Wanted Chicken*), *The Servant Girl's Legacy* (November, with *You Can't Beat Them*. In England the second comedy was *Swami Sam*), *He Wanted His Pants* (December, with *Brown's Cook*. In England the second film was *Love and Limberger*), *Dobs at the Shore* (December, with *He Made His Mark*. In England the second film was *Tale of a Coat*), *The Fresh Air Cure* (December, with Sam and the Bully. The second film in England was *Love and Title*), *Weary Willie's Rags* (December, with *It Cured Hubby*).

1915. *What He Forgot* (January, with *He Gave Him a Million*. In England the second film was *Mr. Stubb's Pen*), *They Looked Alike* (January, with *The New Editor*. In England the second film was *He Made His Mark*), *Spaghetti and the Lottery* (January, with *Mr. Stubb's Pen*. In England the second film was *Who's Who*?), *Gus and the Anarchists* (January, with *Cupid's Target*), *Shoddy the Tailor* (January).

Lubin closes Jacksonville studio on February 13, 1915. The following films, according to Rob Stone, "represent the known backlog of Oliver Hardy's Lubin films. All were produced prior to February 13, 1915."

The Prize (March, with *The Road to Reno*), *An Expensive Visit* (March), *Cleaning Time (*April, with *Black Art*), *Mixed Flats* (April. Released as split reel in England with the film *Haunted Attic*), *Safety Worst* (May, with *The Undertaker's Daughter*. In England the second film was *Perchival's Awakening*), *The Twin Sister* (May, with a cartoon *Cursed! Jack Dalton!*), *Who Stole the Doggies?* (May, with a cartoon called *A Hot Time in Punkville*. In England this cartoon was replaced by *Caught With the Goods*), A Lucky Strike, *Matilda's Legacy* (May),*Capturing Bad Bill* (June, with *Caught with the Goods*), *Her Choice* (June), *The Cannibal King* (July, with a cartoon called *Ping Pong Woo*), *What a Cinch* (July, with a cartoon called *Studies in Clay*), *The Dead Letter* (August, with the cartoon *Persistent Dalton*), *Avenging Bill* (August, with *Avenging Bill* and a cartoon called *Mile-A-Minute Monty*.), *The Haunted Hat* (August, with *Avenging Bill* and the cartoon *Mile-A-Minute Monty*. In England *Avenging Bill* and the cartoon *Monty* were replaced by *An African Hunt*), *Babe's School Days* (September, with the cartoon *Wandering Bill*), *Edison Bugg's Invention* (July, with *Under the Barrel*), *A Terrible Tragedy* (July, with *The Rival Queens*), *It Happened in Pikersville* (July).

NOTES

1. *Florida Times Union*, Lubin Company to Return to Jacksonville, October 8,1912, p.11
2. *Florida Times-Union*, March 21, 1912, page 13, section 2, column 3.
3. Rob Stone, in *Laurel or Hardy*, notes that a backlog of Lubin films would keep Hardy seemingly appearing with Lubin through mid 1916, although his association with Lubin actually ended February 13, 1915. See Stone pages 2, 18, 61-62, 86-93, and a listing of these films on pages 62-85 of Stone's book. . . . The chronology used here in film listings rely on information provided in *Laurel or Hardy*.

Chapter Four

Vim Comedy Company

The Vim Comedy Company players leased the former Lubin studio, at 740-750 Riverside Avenue, in November of 1915. Vim came to Jacksonville from Bayonne, New Jersey—where they'd filmed at the former Avenue E and East 43rd Street Centaur studio.

The Jacksonville studio building had originally housed the Florida Yacht Club, although Vim leased it from the Lubin Company. The *Florida Times Union*, of November 4, 1915, notes the original lease was only for the winter.

Mark Dintenfass was Vim's treasurer. His office was at 1600 Broadway and 326 Lexington Avenue, New York City. General Manager and Director General Louis Burstein was in charge of the Jacksonville studio. His wife, Mildred Burstein, was his secretary.

In a unique Sunday Times-Union article in the January 16, 1916 issue, section 3, page 5, the Vim Studio was described. "Scenes at the Vim Studio" had the following to say. . . .

The Vim moving picture studio on Riverside avenue is one of the most modern to be found anywhere in the South, and when a Times-Union dropped in a few days ago to look over things he found it one of the busiest places in Jacksonville. With two companies at work in the studio and one just returning from a trip about the city, where several scenes were made; with the call of the directors and sound of the hammer and saw, things were quite lively behind the high board fence.

When the newspaperman stepped within the front door he was met by Miss Mildred Burstein, secretary, who escorted him through the big plan to the outside stage, where General Manager Louis Burstein was looking after the details of several scenes being made. Once in the hands of the general manager, the scribe was taken from point to point within the large enclosure, from the open-air stage to the drying room, where the big drying cylinder was unrolling reel after reel of newly made scenes. The dark rooms, electrical department and 'load' rooms are modern in every respect, and things are conducted in clock-like manner by the various men in charge of each department.

In the foregoing picture layout will be seen Bobby Burns, Ethel Burton, Robin Williamson and Spook Hanson working under the direction of Director W.H. Stull, while James L. Carlton was turning the crank at the camera. If all scenes in this comedy areas laughable as the one seen by the newspaper man, the public will be well pleased with what they see on the screen.

General Manager Burstein was found to be a most genial gentleman, and although a busy man, gave up his time to explain the workings of the plant to the scribe.

The Vim Company is occupying the studio formerly occupied by the Lubin Company, having leased the plant for seven years, and Manager Burstein declares he will keep companies at work here all year round.

The personnel of the three companies now at work in the big studio is as follows:

General Manager. Louis Burstein: secretary, Miss Mildred Burstein: directors, Walter H. Stull, Robert Burns, Edward McQuade, Will Louis. Assistant directors are Harry Narthton, Bert Tracey, Roy Gahres and Ernest Boehm.

Star men. Bobby Burns, Babe Hardy, Billy Ruge, Fernando Perez, Robbin Williamson, Billy Bletcher, Spook Hansen, James H. Schroed and Joe Cohen.

Star women, Elsie McLeod, Ethel Burton, Edna Reynolds, Florence McLaughton and Helen Gilmore.

Acting people, men. Harry Byrnes, Walter Baker and George Marks.

Women. Anna Mingus, Arline Roberts and Violet Burnes.

Cameramen, James L. Carlton, Al Ausbacher, H.E. Partridge, Howard Green.

Carpenters—W.O. Jelf, P.M. Jones, A.L. Stokes.

Stage Men—C.V. Sherwood, Vernon Eldert, Clarence Fisk, F.J. Wagner, and Emory Burhardt.

Property and Technical Men—Daniel Stull, in charge: Emory Hampton and John Gray, assistants.

Scenic artist, Bruno Ulm. Chauffeur, Henry Hard.

The Vim Company's studio occupies a space 150 by 450 feet, running from Riverside Avenue to the waterfront.

The exterior stage is 52 by 125 feet, with tops and riggings for proper effects.

The company's films are released on the General Film program, as the Vim comedy films entitled Pokes and Jabbs, Plump and Runt and Mr. Bingles.

The interior of the studio is artificially lighted so that close-up scenes can be made to better advantage.

The company is now spending in Jacksonville, in regular salaries, approximately $3.300 weekly. In addition to this a great number of 'extras' are used, which quite often runs up as high as $400 per week. In all, the Vim Company is paying out, in cash money, approximately $3,800 weekly, all of which is circulated in Jacksonville.

At the far end of the lot the newspaper man found a bunch of carpenters at work enlarging the open air stage, this work now being practically completed. In others sections of the lot can be found small buildings, representing stores etc.

General Manager Burstein is delighted with Jacksonville, and declares he has never before run into such a congenial set of people. He declares he is meeting with encouragement from all sides, which naturally makes him want to remain here permanently.

Jacksonville's *Sunday Metropolis* newspaper (February 20, 1916, page 5C) notes that Burnstein was a Brooklyn lawyer before becoming involved with the film industry. While working in Jacksonville at Vim, Burstein spelled out his feelings about comedy filmmaking in these words...

I have studied the problem of how to produce good comedies thoroughly and into Vim films I am putting the entire result of my studies and experiences. I say the problem of good comedies' because it is a problem. It is much harder to make people laugh than to make them cry, but, nevertheless, I have resolved that every Vim release shall be a side splitter.

This is the prescription I am following that I think will make Vim comedies speedily triumph. First of all, every one of our comedies must have a plot. Although slapstick in nature, we must not insult the intelligence of our audiences by making the film a hodgepodge.

We are going to demonstrate that slapstick comedies can have a plot. Secondly, our comedies must be clean. We will not, and have not tolerated vulgarity. There is nothing in our pictures that one needs be ashamed to laugh at. We have hired only the best talent, and have spared no expense in the making of our film.

Over time the personnel at the Vim Comedy Company included: Directors: Walter H. Stull, Robert "Bobby" Burns, Edward McQuade, Will Louis, Oliver Hardy. Assistant Directors: Harry Narthon, Bert Tracey, Roy Gahres, Ernest Boehm. Male Stars: Oliver Hardy, Billy Ruge, Walter H. Stull, Robert "Bobby" Burns, Fernandez Perez, Robbin Williamson, Billy Fletcher, Spook Hansen, James S. Schroed, Joe Cohen, Harry Myers. Female Stars: Elsie MacLeod, Ethel Burton, Edna Reynolds, Florence McLaughlin, Helen Gilmore, Kate Price, Rosemary Theby. Supporting players: Harry Burnes, Violet Burnes, Walter Baker, George Marks, Anna Mingus, and Arline Roberts. Cameramen: James L. Carlton, Al Ausbacher, H.E. Partridge, Hopward Green, Herman O'Brock, Harry L. "Happy" Keepers.

By June of 1916 Vim's success had led to their year round filming in Jacksonville, with three film company units. These were: Pokes and Jabbs, Plump and Runt (Oliver Hardy and Billy Ruge), and Mr. Bungles (Fernandez Perez). The studio extended from Riverside Avenue to the waterfront. (Sunday Metropolis, June 4, 1916, page 8.)

Pokes and Jabbs (Bob Burns and Walter Stull) were Vim's original comedy stars. They had worked at the Wizard Film Company in early 1915, which had been started by Burstein. When the Equitable Film Company

Figure 4.1. Oliver Hardy & Kate Price of the Vim Comedy Company (Florida State Archives).

Figure 4.2. Pearl Bailey, Budd Ross, "Babe" Oliver Hardy, Ethel Burton, 1916 (Florida State Archives).

Figure 4.3. Kate Price, Actress for Vim Studios (Florida State Archives).

Figure 4.4. The Moving Picture World, April 1, 1916.

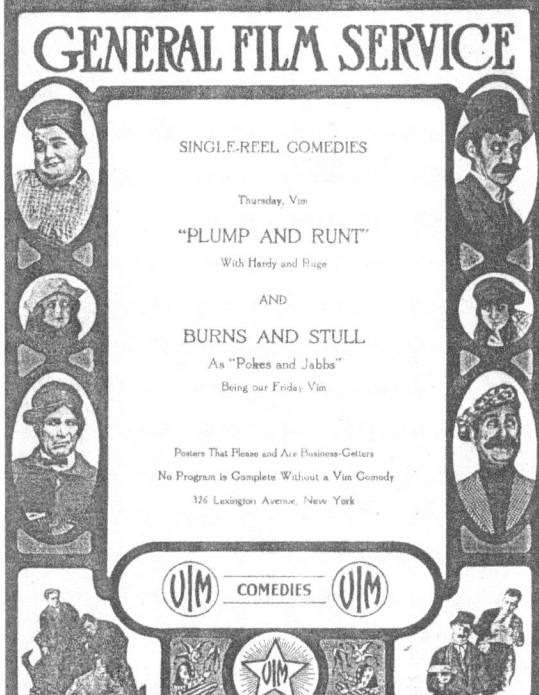

Figure 4.5. Comedians Burns & Stull (Jacksonville Historical Society).

Figure 4.6. Comedians Burns & Stull (Florida State Archives).

Figure 4.7. Comedians Burns & Stull (Jacksonville Historical Society).

bought Wizard, Burstein started Vim, with financing through the Melies Film Company.

An article, in the Florida Metropolis, of February 20, 1916 (page 5) describes the team. It is titled *"Burns and Stull: The Original Laugh Getters"*. . . .

> Walter Stull, who takes the part of Mr. Pokes, began his theatrical career in stock. Starring in Philadelphia in 1894 with the Forepaugh Stock Company, Stull instantly achieved local popularity and left this first engagement to take the leading stock roles at the Girard Avenue Theater, in Philadelphia. After enjoying the idea of being a matinee idol there for many years, he went on the road as co-star of *Emma Bunting* , followed by several seasons as the juvenile in the dramatic company headed by Creaton Clark.
>
> In 1907 he decided to strike out for himself, and for two seasons headed the Walter H. Stull Stock Company. But an attractive offer from the Lubin Company lured him to the 'screen,' and while there he met 'Bobby Burns.'
>
> Bobby Burns made his stage debut as an acrobatic comedian, playing the leading vaudeville houses in Europe and America. At the completion of his vaudeville engagement he played for three seasons in the original 'Babes in Toyland' company, and later in 'The Wizard of Oz.' He also played in 'Ziegfeld Follies,' and from there went with Selig and then Lubin.

Oliver Hardy had just barely started his film career, and was years away from the fame he'd later achieve when paired with Stan Laurel under the auspices of Hal Roach. *The Florida Metropolis*, of February 20, 1916, page 5-C, notes. . . .

> About three years ago when Lubin was looking around for a fat comedian, he chose from among several very prominent heavy weights Babe Hardy, a well known vaudeville performer. Babe came up to all expectations and qualifications of the type for which he was selected, as he weighed over three hundred and fifty pounds, as six feet nine inches in height and at that time only nineteen years of age.
>
> He was at once cast for leading parts with the Lubin Comedy Company, where he made a very enviable record for himself, not only being a very capable actor, but despite his weight was extremely agile, and some of the falls which he has made have astonished and delighted audiences wherever his pictures have been shown.
>
> Last year Mr. Hardy left the Lubin Company to join Wharton Bros. Inc. where he was featured in the 'Get Rich Wallingford Series.' Last fall when the Vim Film Company was organized, Mr. Hardy was one of the first actors to be engaged by Mr. Burstein, who had seen the fat fellow perform, and had recognized his worth to the company. Mr. Hardy is now known as Mr. Plump in the now famous Plump and Runt series, which are being produced by the Vim Film Corporation and released on the General Film program. Mr. Hardy is a Southern boy, claiming Georgia as his native State, and has a host of friends not only throughout the South, but throughout the entire country.

The Sunday Metropolis lists the Plump and Runt cast as including: Bert Tracey, Billy Bletcher, Helen Gilmore, Ethel Burton and Harry Burns. As of December 1916, Herman O'Brock was filming the comedies in which Oliver Hardy appeared. Will Louis directed the Plump and Runt comedies.

Will Louis had started his career at Lubin studios—where he worked for twelve years. He next directed films at Edison Company, before joining Vim as comedy director.

The last Plump and Runt comedy was completed around September 25, 1916. It was at this point that Burstein went to Providence, Rhode Island where Myers and Theby were filming. When he returned to Jacksonville Oliver Hardy had been signed to star in a series of comedies with Kate Price.

By May of 1916 Vim was also making domestic comedies starring Harry C. Myers and Rosemary Theby. Myers also directed these comedies, which were filmed by Harry L. "Happy" Keepers. *The Moving Picture World*, of May 6, 1916, page 949, noted that "for his first release, Mr. Myers has chosen a story which offers opportunity for some elaborate effects as well as sparkling comedy. He practically owned the outdoor stage last week,

Figure 4.8. Rosemary Theby (Blair Miller Collection). Credit: Wisconsin Center for Film and Theater Research.

Figure 4.9. Harry Myers (Blair Miller Collection). Credit: Wisconsin Center for Film and Theater Research.

and this gives some idea of the scope of the work, for the stage comprises 35,000 square feet under cloth diffusers. No date has yet been set for the first release, but advance bookings have already been received from all parts of the country."

Vim comedies were released through the General Film Company. They revolved around the series of Pokes and Jabbs, Plump and Runt, and the domestic comedies Harry Myers and Rosemary Theby. When Plump and Runt plots wore thin, Hardy was paired in comedies with Kate Price. Price had come to Vim from Vitagraph. Vim closed in 1917, bringing to an end the Hardy-Price collaboration.

The final days of the Vim Comedy Company present an unclear picture. It is known that problems with the Vim employee payroll, as identified by Oliver Hardy, contributed to its demise. It is also apparent that Louis Burstein and Mark Dintenfass started over—with certain of the former Vim staff going with Burstein and others going with Dintenfass.

Louis Burstein was left with the nucleus of what would become the King-Bee Films Corporation. This included Oliver "Babe" Hardy, Ethel Burton, Florence McLoughlin, Joe Cohen, Budd Ross and cameraman Herman O'Brock. Initially they were the Babe Hardy Company. As King-Bee they would add Billy West, Arvid E. Gillstrom, Polly Van and Ethlynn Gibson.

The Dintenfass contingent emerged under the auspices of Amber Star Comedies—which included Pokes and Jabbs (Burns and Stull), Billy Ruge, Kate Price and director Will Louis. Subsequently Amber Star was renamed—becoming Jaxon Comedies—producers of Pokes and Jabbs, Sparkle Comedies and comedies starring Kate Price.

The July 7, 1917 (page 23) issue of Motography carried a story entitled "Debut of Sparkle Comedies" which described these comedies in the following way....

> The Sparkle Comedies are an innovation in one reel comedies, and are best described as to their tendency by the name. They are given to sprightly plots farcical in their complications and demanding true humor and good acting throughout. They are, however, described as thoroughly refined and of a nature calculated to prove a boon to houses that want fun without robustness. It is predicted by General Film officials that these 'Sparkle Comedies' will make new stars in a field that is woefully underrepresented, that of light comedy in motion pictures.
>
> The 'Sparkle Comedies' are from the studios of the Jaxon Film Co., which has already been producing several series of favorite subjects. These releases are to be had in groups of six and the first group includes 'Where Is My Nighty?' 'Fresh Air,' 'The Spy,' 'The Trunk Route,' 'The Water Cure' and 'Night of Enchantment.'

Both groups initially filmed at Vim's former Riverside Avenue facility—but the Amber Star group later moved (circa November, 1916) to Jacksonville's Garrick studios.

POKES AND JABBS COMEDIES FILMOGRAPHY WITH ROBERT PAUL "BOBBY" BURNS AND WALTER STULL

1915. *Midnight Prowlers* (November), *A Pair of Birds* (November), *Pressing Business* (November), *Strangled Harmony* (December), *Speed Kings* (December), *Mixed and Fixed* (December), *Ups and Downs* (December). 1916. *This Way Out* (January), *Chickens (January), Frenzied Finance (January), Busted Hearts (January), The Getaway (February), The High Sign* (February), *Pluck and Luck* (February), *Love and Lather* (February), *A Pair of Skins* (March), *Behind the Footlights* (March), *Anvils and Actors* (March), *In the Ring* (April), *The Sleuths* (April), *Hired and Fired* (April),*Home Made Pies* (May), *The Pretenders* (May), *A Fair Exchange* (May), *Villains and Violins* (May), *The Land Lubbers* (June), *A Dollar Down* (June), *The Sea Dogs* (June), *Hungry Hearts* (June),*The Raid* (June), *For Better or Worse* (June), *For Value Received* (June), *Furnished Rooms* (July), *The Great Safe Tangle* (July), *Help!Help!* (July), *Wait a Minute* (August), *Rushing Business* (August), *Comrades* (August), *Dreamy Knights* (August), *The Try-Out* (August), *Lifesavers* (August), *A Bag of Troubles* (September), *Love and Duty* (September), *The Reward* (September), *Payment-in-Full* (September),*The Reformers* (September), *Strictly Business* (October), *The Frame-Up* (October), *Watch Your Watch* (October), *Here and There* (October), *In the Ranks* (November), *Hot Dogs* (November), *Good and Proper* (November), *Money-Maid Man* (November), *Ambitious Ethel* (December),*A Rare Boarder* (December), *What's the Use ?* (December).1917. *War Correspondents* (January).

PLUMP AND RUNT COMEDIES FILMOGRAPHY WITH OLIVER HARDY AND BILLY RUGE

1916. *A Special Delivery* (January), *A Sticky Affair* (February), *One Too Many* (February), *The Serenade* (March), *Nerve and Gasoline* (March), *Their Vacation* (March), *Momma's Boy* (April), *A Royal Battle* (April), *All for a Girl* (April), *What's Sauce for the Goose* (April. with Kate Price and Elsie MacLeod), *The Brave Ones* (May. with Billy Bletcher and Elsie MacLeod), *The Water Cure* (May. with Elsie MacLeod), *Thirty Days* (May. with Elise MacLeod), *Baby Doll* (May), *The Schemers* (June), *Never Again* (June), *Bet-

ter Halves (June), *A Day at School* (July), *Spaghetti* (July), *Aunt Bill* (July. with Billy Bletcher), *The Heroes* (July), *Human Hounds* (August), *Their Honeymoon* (August), *An Aerial Joyride* (August), *Side-Tracked* (September), *Stranded* (September), *Royal Blood* (October), *The Candy Trail* (October), *A Precious Parcel* (October).

VIM COMEDIES FILMOGRAPHY WITH
HARRY C. MYERS AND ROSEMARY THEBY

1916. *Housekeeping* (July), *Hubby's Relative* (August), *That Tired Businessman* (August), *Their Dream House* (August), *The Tormented Husband* (August), *The Chalk Line* (September), *His Strenuous Visit* (September), *Artistic Atmosphere* (September), *A Grain of Suspicion* (October), *Their Installment Furniture* (October), *Green Eyes* (October), *A Persistent Wooing* (October), *Gertie's Garters* (November), *Marked "No Fund"* (November), *His Wedding Promise* (November), *The Good Stenographer* (November), *Hubby's Chicken* (November), *Charity Begins at Home* (December), *They Practice Economy* (December), *Her Financial Frenzy* (December). 1917. *It's All Wrong* (January).

VIM COMEDIES FILMOGRAPHY
OLIVER HARDY WITH KATE PRICE

Price came to Vim after working at Vitagraph and then Triangle-Keystone. 1916. *A Maid to Order* (October. cast included Raymond McKee, who had worked with Hardy at both Lubin and Edison), *Twin Flats* (November), *A Warm Reception* (November), *Pipe Dreams* (November), *Mother's Child* (November), *The Prizewinners* (November), *The Guilty Ones* (December. Billy Ruge's last film appearance with Oliver Hardy. Subsequently Ruge moved to Amber Star / Jaxon—where Will Louis directed him in comedies), *He Winked and Won* (December. with Ethel Burton), *Fat and Fickle* (December. with Ethel Burton). 1917. *The Love bugs* (January. with Ethel Burton), *The Boycotted Baby* (January), *The Other Girl* (January).

VIM COMEDIES FILMOGRAPHY
WITH FERNANDO PEREZ AS BUNGLES

1916. *Bungles Rainy Day* (February), *Bungles Enforces the Law* (February), *Bungles Elopement* (March), *Bungles Lands a Job* (March).

Chapter Five

Amber Star Company and the Eastern Film Company

The Amber Star Company was located at South Jacksonville's Garrick studios at Dixieland Park, on Eighth Street, and was owned by the Eastern Film Corporation of Providence, Rhode Island. With the demise of the Vim studio Amber Star had acquired most of its assets and moved these assets to the Garrick studios, located at Dixieland Park.

Dixieland Park was originally an amusement park across the St. John River from Jacksonville and had become home to a number of independent studios. Before Amber Star, previous tenants had included the Monograph Company of America (1910)—the first film company to rent space at Dixieland—and the Selig Polyscope Company, which moved into the Motograph studio space when Motograph went out of business.

The *Florida Times Union* described the circumstances of this move more fully in a November 7, 1916 article, on page 14, entitled "Old Vim Concern Bawled Up In Finances." In the subsequent text of the article it is stated....

The Amber Star Film Corporation, which was formerly the Vim Company, yesterday moved its quarters from the old Lubin studio in Riverside to the Garrick Studios Company's plant in South Jacksonville, according to announcement made by Frank A. Tichenor of the former concern, who is here investigating affairs of the local branch. He declared last night that the Garrick Studios will be used until later, when his firm intends to erect a private studio on a suitable location.

According to Mr. Tichenor, who came here from the home offices of Amber Star Film Corporation at Providence , R.I., the financial affairs of the local; branch are in a muddled condition, and steps are being taken to straighten them out. He declared that there is large shortage of company money, which is being traced by company auditors now working on the books.

While Mr. Tichenor did not go into details as to the company's affairs, he declared that the shortages were thought to have been caused by padding of payrolls and redating of old accounts paid against the Vim Company by local concerns.

Mark Dintenfass (former partner of Louis Burstein in the Vim Comedy Company) headed the former Vim contingent which left Riverside Avenue for the Amber Star. Others included Walter Stull, Bobby Burns, Billy Ruge and Kate Price. Will Louis directed the Amber Star comedies. Frank A. Tichenor, Eastern's business manager, created Jaxon Film Company in Jacksonville, which made three principle comedy series: Sparkle comedies, Pokes and Jabs comedies and Finn and Haddie comedies. All were made under the auspices of Amber- Star. Subsequently Tichenor and the Amber Star Company, called an end to Jaxon's Jacksonville filmmaking—moving everything back to Providence, Rhode Island.

Tichenor had entered the film business after coming to New York City from Kentucky. Initially engaged in the business of producing and distributing stereopticon slides, he had used $30,000 of the profits to buy an interest in the General Film Company.

General was a film distribution company formed by the Motion Picture Patent Companies (Kleine, Melies, Kalem, Pathe, Edison, Biograph, Vitagraph, Lubin, Selig and Essanay companies) to distribute the films made by its member companies.

When the Sherman Antitrust Act (and various other related developments in the film industry) threatened the demise of the General Film Company, and its parent Motion Picture Patents Company, Tichenor stepped in to try and rescue his investment (and those of the other General Film investors).

Recognizing his managerial skills, and good intentions, Tichenor was made executive vice-president and general manager of the General Film Company. He cut costs, and succeeded in saving both his investment and the investments of the men who had put him in charge at the General Film Company.

As a result, Frank H. Hitchcock, General Film's legal counsel (and former postmaster-general of President Taft's administration) and Republican National Committeeman Frederick S. Peck became Tichenor's close friends. Both men were among the General Film investors who had their investments, in General Film, saved by Tichenor.

On the eve of the collapse of General Film, Tichenor started the Photo Play Productions Company, and soon after had joined Frederick S. Peck in starting the Eastern Film Corporation. Eastern's studio was at Providence, Rhode Island, at the former General Film studio which Peck owned. The partners used Tichnor's Photo Play Productions offices, in New York City at 220 West 42nd Street, as the business offices.[1] The twenty-three story building, built by Coca-Cola magnate Asa Candler, was called the Candler Building. It was ideal for Eastern, as it housed cutting rooms and storage vaults approved by the National Board of Fire Underwriters and New York City for a filmmaking business.

Eastern had a small Providence office at 1100 Elmwood Avenue, while the studio was at 1-17 McKinley Street. Frederick S. Peck, a Republican millionaire from Barrington, Rhode Island, owned the Eastern Company. In 1914 he became interested in movies as a way of adding to his wealth and power. . Eastern was incorporated in December of 1914, but did not actually start filming movies until May of 1915. Their most prolific filmmaking years were 1916 and 1917. Peck was not interested in supervising the day-to-day managing of the studio, which he left to general manager and director Elwood I. Bostwich. As previously stated, Frank A. Tichenor was Eastern's business manager.

Eastern's Providence studio was apparently very successful. Newspaper reports, in 1915, noted there were. . . .

> Over 40 players at work. These are divided into three groups, each with a special director and each doing a picture. As fast as one picture is done, another is begun...The studio is large enough for three sets at one time. In other words, three directors can put on three scenes simultaneously and none will be interfering with each other. In summer when it is too hot to work indoors, interior scenes will be taken on the outdoor stage, which is in the yard behind the old brewery building. This stage will hold five sets without crowding. Its sides and top will be covered with white muslin curtains which will diffuse the light so that there will be no shadows. Any kind of scene may be made as easily as indoors.[2]

In the aftermath of the move back to Providence, it was not long before Eastern abandoned comedies all together—and concentrated on industrial and social service films.

Then, on August 23, 1917, a fire at the studio brought an end to even that—destroying the stage building and Providence's claim to be a center of movie production activity.

NOTES

1. The former tenant of this office space was Joseph Miles, the younger brother of Harry, Herbert and Earl C. Miles—who had formed the Miles Brothers Motion Picture Company in San Francisco. This company is described more fully in *American Silent Film Comedies: An Illustrated Encyclopedia of Persons, Studios and Terminology*, by Blair Miller and *The Golden Gate and the Silver Screen*, by Geoffrey Bell. Both books are detailed more fully in the bibliography.

2. As mentioned in the Providence *Sunday Journal*, February 7, 1971, page 4.

Chapter Six

King-Bee Film Corporation

In the aftermath of the Vim Comedy Company breakup, Louis B. Burstein started the King-Bee Film Corporation. Filming was initially at the former Vim studio (740-750 Riverside Avenue), then relocated to Bayonne, New Jersey (late summer, 1917) and finally to 1329 Gordon Street, Hollywood, California.

King-Bee had New York City offices, according to an April 28, 1917 ad in *The Moving Picture World,* at 924 Longacre Building at Forty-second and Broadway. N.H. Spitzer was the sales manager; Louis Burstein, president and general manager; L.L. Hiller, treasurer; Herman Obrock, photographer; and Arvid E. Gillstrom the general studio director. Ads noted Gillstrom was "formerly director of Charlie Chaplin and many Keystone comedies" and promised "Laughs that Linger, Roars that Reverberate...Two reel Films presenting Billy West, The Funniest Man on the Continent."

In the May 25, 1917 issue of Variety (Volume 46, page 23), the first three King Bee comedies were reviewed. . . .

> The first three comedies made by the King Bee Film Corp., starring Billy West, were shown privately last week. The new company is turning out comedies in two reels each, and is following closely upon comedy ideas employed by Chaplin. West follows the work of the Mutual comedy minutely with the main bits of comedy consisting of the messy work which has marked the Keystone and other makes of comedies. The first three King Bee productions have evidently been copied from pictures made by Chaplin, especially the one entitled 'Dough,' which resembles the Keystone 'Dough and Dynamite,' one of the best pictures ever made by Chaplin. The other two King Bees are entitled 'Back Stage' and 'The Hero.' Both abound in rough comedy material and from the general appearance should prove laugh-provokers in the houses which cannot afford to get the new Chaplins. In addition to the star the casts for the three pictures include

Figure 6.1. Arvid Gillstrom with Ethel Burton Palmer (Jacksonville Historical Society).

Babe Hardy, Leo White, Budd Ross, Ethel Burton, Florence McLoughlin and Joe Cohan. Arvid E. Gillstrom did the directing under the surpervision of Louis Burstein, with camera work by Herman Osbrock.

King-Bee made a total of five Billy West Comedies at the former Vim Jacksonville studio, beginning in March of 1917. According to Rob Stone, author of *Laurel or Hardy* there were five King-Bee comedies made in Jacksonville, of which Backstage was the first. All of these films were two-reels in length, produced by Burstein, directed by Arvid Gillstrom, filmed by Herman Obrock and edited by Ben H. Cohen. *The Moving Picture World*, in an article from the June 2, 1917 issue, page 1453, profiled Billy West with these words. . . .

> Billy West, the volatile and versatile young comedian of King-Bee Comedies, has achieved screen popularity at a bound. He is the life and soul of "Back Stage," about which everyone is talking.
>
> Young West has been on the stage since boyhood. He won fame in Chicago as a cartoonist and singer, and came to be known, as his experience lengthened, as "The Boy Judge." He has played in all the leading vaudeville houses and

theaters of the United States, and has acquired a vogue and popularity which focuses attention upon him now that he has entered the broad field of the picture.

In addition to "Backstage," the first King-Bee offering shortly to be shown, Billy West appears in two other comedies now nearing completion. He has a brisk, alert, spontaneous, but natural, form of humor and achieves his effects without much apparent effort. His success is the result of hard work and a thorough mastery of stage and screen craft. At this time when innate ability on the screen secures wide plaudits, Billy West's acceptable efforts reflect favorably upon Louis Burstein, president and general manager of the King-Bee Films, and his able director, Arvid Gillstrom.

Billy West's fund of originality in screen work will, in due time, have the widest possible opportunities of revealing itself for the delectation of his large circle of admirers.

Stone mentions that the other King-Bee comedies made in Jacksonville were:

- *The Hero*. Released June 1, 1917. States rights release. 2 reel. No copyright registered. Cast: Billy West, Babe Hardy, Ethel Burton, Leo White, Budd Ross, Polly Van, Florence McLoughlin, Frank Lasneer, Ben Ross, Joe Cohen, Frank Bates. This film compared to Chaplin's *Caught in a Cabaret*.
- *Dough-Nuts*. Released June 15, 1917. State rights. 2 reel. No copyright registered. aka. The Bakery. Cast: Billy West, Ethel Burton, Babe Hardy, Leo White, Budd Ross, Florence McLoughlin, Joe Cohen, Frank Bates. This film compared to Chaplin's *Dough and Dynamite*.
- *Cupid's Rival*. Released July 1, 1917. States rights. 2 reel. No copyright registered. Cast: Billy West, Babe Hardy, Ethel Burton, Leo White, Budd Ross, Joe Cohne, Ethlyn Gibson, Florence McLoughlin. Stone notes that Gibson, who had appeared in West's Unicorn comedies, joined the King-Bee stock company beginning with this film. She remained with West comedies through the late 1920's Artclass and Weiss Brothers comedies.
- *The Villain*. Released July 15, 1917.states rights. 2 reel. No copyright registered. Cast: Billy West, Babe Hardy, Florence McLoughlin, Budd Ross, Ethlyn Gibson, Leo White, Joe Cohen.

Louis Burstein was a key player in a number of silent film companies. His career, up to the time of King-Bee Films Corporation is aptly summarized in the following June 16, 1917 Moving Picture World (page 1729) article. . . .

Consistency is the keynote in the success that has followed Louis Burstein's career in motion pictures. He has always been associated with the production of comedies, and from his first appearance in the moving picture field, when he participated in the organization of the New York Motion Picture Company and the Keystone Film Company, Mr. Burstein's efforts have been concentrated in the making of films that cause laughter.

Figure 6.2. King Bee—Billy West Advertisement (Moving Picture World trade magazine).

After the Keystone Company got under way, Mr. Burstein withdrew for a temporary period and devoted his time to outside interests, but the lure of the studio was strong enough to bring him back. He organized the Wizard Film Company with Burns and Stull as the leading funmakers. This company was absorbed by the Equitable Film Corporation, and Mr. Burstein proceeded to start the company which established itself as prime favorite under the brand Vim Comedies. Under his banner the company was able to make slapstick comedies, on one hand and refined comedies on the other in the same studio at a production cost which was the marvel of his competitors.

When Billy West, the noted funster, became free to make new production connections, he sought a producer and found him in Louis Burstein. The result was the formation of the King-Bee Films Corporation and the signing as director of Arvid E. Gillstrom.

The combination of Louis Burstein, Billy West and Arvid E. Gillstrom, backed by a supporting company including Babe Hardy, Ethel Burton, Florence McLaughlin, Polly Van, Joe Cohan, Bud Ross and Ethlynn Gibson, makes the King-Bee Films Corporation a strong company.

Kalton C. Lahue and Sam Gill, in their 1970 book Clown Princes and Court Jesters, pages 399-400, devote a whole chapter to the subject of Billy West. They describe his Kingbee comedies with the following words. . . .

Figure 6.3. King Bee Film Corporation—Billy West Advertisement (Moving Picture World trade magazine).

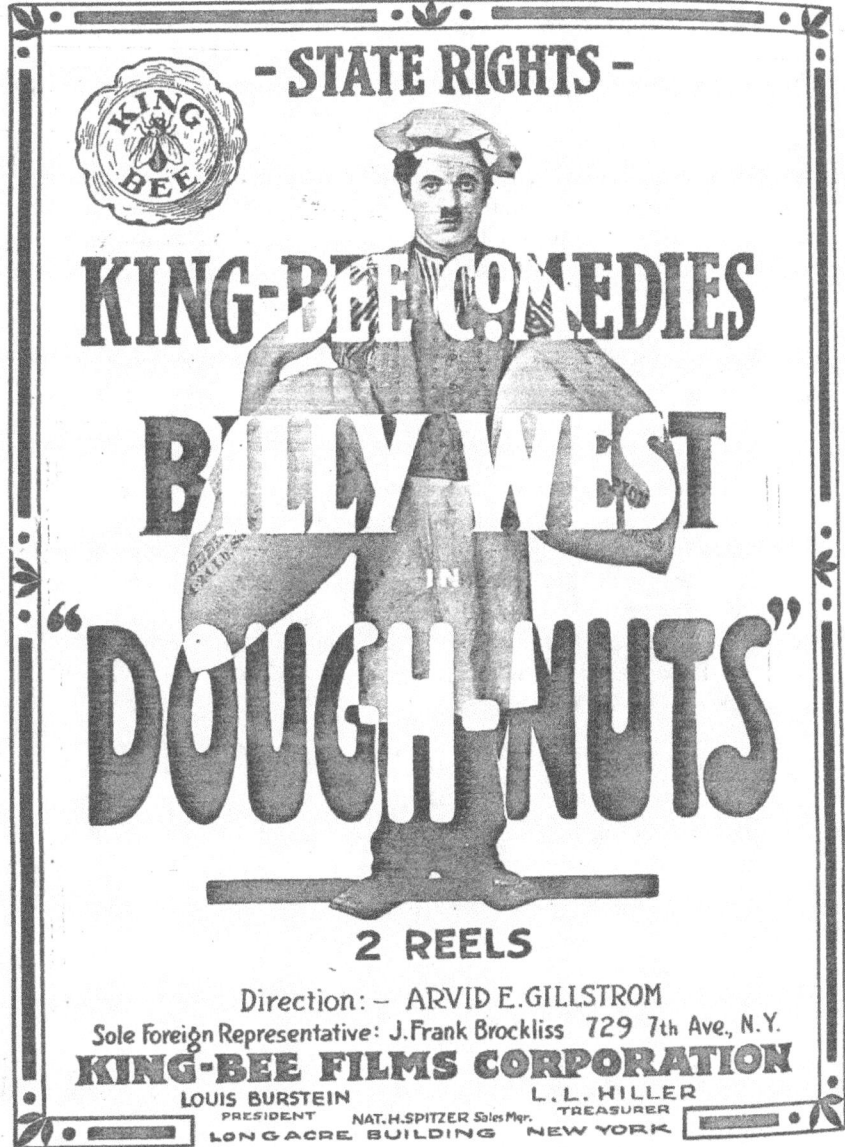

Figure 6.4. King Bee Film Corporation—Billy West Advertisement (Moving Picture World trade magazine).

Billy's King Bee Comedies were made in 1917-18. At this time Chaplin was at Lone Star making his famous series of Mutual-Chaplins. Charlie had entered films in 1914, making thirty-five in a year with Keystone and then doing a series for Essanay in 1915-16 before West started his motion picture career. Thus, Billy had a relatively large number of Chaplin films that he could have modeled his scripts after, but it's to his credit that the Billy West Comedies bore no relation to Chaplin's previous films . . . Billy's tramp was another dimension of Charlie's. Where Chaplin's little fellow exhibited a tendency toward cynicism, tempered with a degree of hopeful optimism (which was always badly bent by the fadeout), Billy's tramp was the cheerful optimist who was treated pretty decently by fate. Most of his problems came about as the result of his own carefree ineptitude.

In an article entitled *West and Bee Swarm Fly West*, the *Moving Picture World*, on page 717 of November 3, 1917 issue described the move to Los Angeles, California...

Louis Burstein has arranged for forthcoming winter-made King-Bee comedies to be produced in sunny California. As a result of his imperial ukase nineteen of the human insects who make honey for the King-Bee Film Corporation departed from the depot of the Lehigh Valley across the Hudson Monday, October 22, bound for Los Angeles. The party traveled in a private car, and in addition to cameramen, carpenters and property men comprised of Director Gillstrom, Billy West, Babe Hardy, Leo White, Bud Ross, Ethel Gibson, Martha Dean, and Jackie Jackson—nineteen in all.

By December of 1917 King-Bee would be firmly relocated in Hollywood—having left Jacksonville, filming briefly in New York City and Bayonne, New Jersey—before heading for Hollywood. They had said a permanent farewell to Jacksonville. In Los Angeles their address would be 1329 Gordon Street.

Chapter Seven

Eagle Film Company

The Eagle Film Manufacturing and Producing Company president and general director, A.S. Roe, and the company manager, H.A. Kelly, came to Jacksonville in late November of 1915 looking for a site to build their studio. They built there studio at 6337 Arlington Road, near Commerce Street, in Arlington Heights.

Both men were from Eagle's 109 North Dearborn Street facility in Chicago, where Eagle's executive offices were located. A site in Jacksonville was chosen by December 2, 1915. According to one source, its structural layout rivaled that of Universal City, California.

In an article titled "Eagle Film Mfg. Co. Has Decided to Build a Big Studio In City," as appeared in the November 28, 1915 issue of the Florida Times Union newspaper it was declared that "Complete Plans Will Be Announced on Arrival of Producing Manager from Chicago." Further it was noted that the "Plant Will be Complete" and "Films Will Be Developed Here. Concern Secures Rights to Forty Comedies." The text provides the following details about this....

> First the Eagle Film Manufacturing and Producing Company of Chicago has decided to take a role in the motion picture world, which will be no small one, and that a most complete and extensive plant will be erected on one of two sites on which the company has options here was the statement last night of A.S. Roe, president of the company.
>
> William J. Dunn, producing manager of the company is now on his way here from Chicago and he with President Roe and H.A. Kelly, general director, will have a conference Tuesday. 'We have closed up all plans to stay but I do not want to state until the arrival of Mr. Dunn where we will be located,' stated Mr. Roe.

The officials state they have secured rights to about forty comedy scenarios by Rex Adams, which will be produced here. Such of the series as have already been put before the public have made big hits. The company will begin producing these features even before the studio is erected.

Yesterday data relative to cost of materials, including lumber, roofing, interior materials for the studio and developing plant were secured by the officials. After the arrival of the producing manager this week, construction work will soon begin.

A specialty of the plant will be the developing of films, either for their own company or others that may be working here. In addition to this a stage of big proportions will be erected. It can be let out to other companies, the facilities of which are inadequate at times.

Mr. Kelly states that he has always liked the lights possible in Florida, and that when he was on the Florida East Coast twenty years ago he was a photographer. This was long before he thought he would be in the motion picture business."

The Florida Times-Union newspaper of December 1915 (12/3/15, page 9, column 1) noted that...

A transaction was closed yesterday whereby the Eagle Film Manufacturing and Producing Company of Chicago acquired a plot of land in Arlington Heights, including a building of considerable size which will be converted into one of the most complete motion picture plants in the South. The purchase was made outright from the Alderman Realty Company. Work of clearing the grounds and making ready for the erection of a mammoth stage, as well as an artificial lake and gardens, has already begun. The concern hopes to have the property ready for one company of movie stars to begin the production of pictures by December 13.

It is the intention of the Eagle people to work three companies here, one producing feature films and two turning out comedies. *The Troubles of Duffy*, an Eagle production which has already won its way to favor in the middle West, will be handled from the Florida point of view by this producing concern.

Officers of the syndicate stated last night that they intend to produce some of the great feature picture plays of the future from their plant here as well.

Located as they will be, just across the St. John's River from the Fairfield section of the city and in easy access of the Arlington ferry, it is the intention of the Eagle people to soon develop a real motion picture facility on its property. An order was placed yesterday for an engine, dynamo and other electrical equipment with the General Electric Company for an individual electric plant. Besides this the company will install its own water system and fire prevention equipment, this supplied by the artesian wells at Arlington Heights.

As soon as the ground is properly cleared and the stumpage removed landscape gardeners will begin their work. The garden feature of the plant will be one of the most important. Superintendent H.A. Kelly stated last night that he would this morning increase the number of laborers at work so as to have the grounds in nominally good shape for the arrival of the first company early this month.

The films of all the pictures made here will also be developed here. The developing plant will be in the charge of Mr. Kelly, who states that the best apparatus known in the manufacturing end of the movie art will be installed. Besides being able to develop their own films Mr. Kelly states that he will cater to other producing companies in this section of the country in developing their films. He believes that this will save them a delay of seventy-two hours in sending their films to New York to be tested out. There are to be retakes this concern will be able to reprise them of the fact without holding the company together for more than a day.

The materials have practically all been contracted for in connection with the great stage and the commodious property house and dressing room. Construction work will be pushed as rapidly as possible, several automobiles have been secured as well as other equipment necessary. President A.J. Roe left last night for Chicago, but will return to Jacksonville within thirty days. William J. Dunn, producing manager of the company, will remain in the city and assist in directing the work.

Further details, about the property, are provided by the publication *Arlington: A New History,* where on page 26 it is stated that "the building it moved into had been constructed the previous year as a cigar factory, at the time a burgeoning industry in Florida. The Alderman Realty Company sold the property in 1913 to R.K. Shaw and H.M. Lott with the provision that the grantees would relocate their cigar business from Quincy, Florida to Arlington and erect a building on the lot for use a cigar factory. The building was to employ 'one hundred and twenty persons five days in each week for a period of three years.' The large frame building, situated at 6337 Arlington Road, may thus have been available when the Eagle Company selected it for a film studio.

Work at Eagle City did proceed rapidly. By the December 16, 1915 issue (page 12, column 2) of the Florida Times-Union, further details were being released...

> The company is erecting three big stages. One of them will be constructed of steel and glass. Bungalows for the actors, directors, cameramen and other employees of the company are also contemplated, including a clubhouse and necessary automobile garages. A complete waterworks system is also to be installed, and everyone connected with the studio will be enrolled in a fire department which is to be organized. There will be an electric light plant to furnish the necessary current for illuminating and power purposes. The equipment for the electric light plant is now arriving. A force of men are now at work building a fireproof vault, where will be stored the valuable completed films.

> The company, ever mindful for the comfort of its employees, has purchased a big motor bus, which will be used to transport the attaches to and from the Arlington ferryboat landing on the river.
>
> Progress of work at the studio will be shown to members of the Jacksonville Chamber of Commerce, who will make a trip to Arlington either tomorrow or Saturday.

The Florida Times Union newspaper, on January 21, 1916, page 13, reported that the Eagle Company had spent $48,000 in building the Arlington studio facility and processing plant. The article reports that H.A. Kelley, Eagle's director general spoke at a lunchtime meeting of the Jacksonville Real Estate Board at the Seminole Hotel, beginning at 12:30 o'clock. He was one of the local motion picture men invited to attend the meeting and tell the members the progress of his industry.

> Mr. Kelly also stated that the plant at Arlington will be ready for operation by the end of the present week and that a total of forty people mostly girls will be employed in the developing and assembling room alone. He stated that all of these will be employed locally with the exception of two who will necessarily have to be experts.
>
> When asked for suggestions as to the improvement of the local industry, he told the realty men that there are two things badly needed for facilitation of the business at Arlington, of which he was necessarily best prepared to talk. These are a new roadway from the plant to the beach road to enable late workers to reach the city without the necessity of a long journey by a circuitous route to the South Jacksonville ferry. He stated that the Arlington ferry ceases operations at 6:45 p.m., which necessarily handicaps late workers. He also stated that telephonic communications with that section was also needed.
>
> The meeting with the board was a brief one. About twenty members were present. In conclusion the body endorsed the mayor's convention and adopted resolutions congratulating Mayor Bowden for calling the conference.

By January 23 of 1916 Jacksonville's *Sunday Metropolis* (page 4) was reporting on the dramatic changes going on at Eagle's Arlington property...

> The Eagle Film Company, who are now establishing in Arlington, across the river, what will be known as the Eagle City have up to the present expended over $40,000 and before they are through, will have invested in this vicinity upwards of $250,000, employing a large number of people, many of whom will be home folks, while they will of course bring their leading ones from New York and Chicago. . . .
>
> At this time there is no way of computing the dollar and cents value of making this the center of moving picture making, as there are so many angles to the business that to try and figure them all out would be impossible, but to get them

here and hold them is the most essential part of the program at this time, and if ever the golden rule should be applied in business, this is the psychological moment, as there is no line of business that will not be either directly or indirectly benefited by their coming and remaining here, and once the actor and actress finds out about what a good place this is to make their permanent home, we will see some of the most beautiful bungalows being built and homes being established that one ever laid eyes upon.

The fact that it is possible to work the entire year, with a loss of a very few days on account of cloudy weather or rain, and that we have a much cooler summer than New York, where there are heat prostration's and sunstroke's galore, all of which we know nothing about, will go a long way in helping to bring producing companies to this city. It is not publicly known but nature provides 'snow' scenes here right now that are far superior to those of the North, while our tropical foliage a few hours ride. We have prairies, jungles and wild scenes of nature that cannot be found anywhere else on the face of the globe. Yet with all these valuable things the importance of giving the picture every assistance cannot be over-estimated.

In June of 1916 the Eagle Film Manufacturing Company became the Eagle Film Company and officially moved to Jacksonville. Here, in 1916, they produced Tweedledum and Tweedledee comedies featuring Fernandez Perez as Tweedledum and wife Babette as Tweedledee. These comedies were distributed by the Unity Sales Corporation, which operated from the New York City Godfrey Building. Yet according to the book Jacksonville's *Architectural Heritage Landmarks for the Future*, "within a year after the Eagle Studios opened, the entire movie industry in Jacksonville began a rapid decline."

Background information about Ferdinand Perez is provided in a short article, in the April 30, 1916 issue of the *Florida Metropolis* newspaper, page 12C, entitled "Ferdinand Perez as Tweedledum in an Eagle Production in which he plays fourteen characters". . . .

> Ferdinand Perez, better known as Tweedledum, plays fourteen different parts in this picture and does it with such ease that one seeing the picture can hardly believe his own eyes.
>
> Ferdinand is a native of sunny Italy, and having been in this country for a short while, speaks only broken English, but he discounts his deficiency in speech by his proficiency in acting. In one scene he plays the wife, the husband, the sweetheart of the wife, the game warden. . . . He appeared on the screen at the same time in all these parts. He plays golf with himself acting as caddy and golfer, and does things that if they were not true would not be believed.
>
> Tweedledum was caught by Billy Dunn of the Eagle Company, who at once began teaching him the American idea of comedy. It was a hard job as Tweedledum continued to adhere to the Continental conception of things funny,

but finally the teacher was successful as the first production of Tweedledum has shown.

This remarkable actor enjoys the reputation of having appeared in more comedy pictures during his screen career than any other movie actor.

His motion picture career was started in Italy, where at Torin he was general director of the famous Ambrostar Company. He came to America with the Eclipse Company and joined the Éclair Company, making the latter famous in its day. . . .Since joining the Eagle players at Arlington he has worked incessantly on various productions, which will be released as soon as possible by the company, and it was announced Saturday by Mr. Dunn that in the future Ferdinand Perez was the director general of all comedy pictures produced by the Eagle people.

Subsequent to Eagle, Perez next worked at the Vim Comedy Company. At Vim his screen character was named Bungles.

The November 25, 1916 issue (page 1211) of Motography carried a short announcement about the release of the first of the Tweedledum comedies. . . .

The Unity Sales Corporation announces the release of its first Tweedledum Comedy, entitled 'Lend Me Your Wife.' This is a two-reel comedy and there is not a dull moment or any let-up to the fun in the adventures of Tweedledum." One version of events concerning the sale of the Eagle property has this to say. . . .

"In 1920 the grounds of the Eagle Film Company were purchased, by Richard E. Norman—who operated the Norman Film Manufacturing Company here from 1920 to 1928. The Norman Film Company made eight feature films here and some film shorts as well, and was distinctive for its all black cast. Norman was a white man. According to his son Richard Norman, Jr., The Norman Company portrayed black family life much like The Cosby Show did on television. "At a time when movies portrayed black people as menacing villains, ignorant savages or simple-minded rustics, Jacksonville's Richard E. Norman was one of the few filmmakers portraying black people as lovers, heroes and entrepreneurs.

The book *Jacksonville's Architectural Heritage: Landmarks for the Future*, gives an alternative version of events. . . .

In 1922 Richard E. Norman purchased the bankrupt Eagle Studios and continued production into the 1930's. Norman Studios primarily made short-subject features, filmed in the Northeast and Midwest, and adventure movies featuring all-black casts, many of which were filmed at the Arlington facility. After Norman retired in 1952, his wife Gloria continued to use the facility as a dance studio until the mid-1970's. This site, with the five wooden buildings from the old movie studio still remaining, is significant as a reminder of Jacksonville's rise and demise as a major movie-making center.

EAGAL FILM COMPANY FILMOGRAPHY

Tweedledum and Tweedledee comedies (released between July 3 and December 11 of 1916):

Tweedledum Torpedoed by Cupid, Tweedledum Plays the Hero, Tweedledum's Busy Night, A Lucky Tramp, Lend Me Your Wife, A Bathtub Elopement, A Shortsighted Crime, Somewhere in Mexico, The Burlesque Show, Tweedledum's Scrambled Honeymoon.

Chapter Eight

Thanhouser Company

The Thanhouser Company was based in New Rochelle, New York. Its Jacksonville studio located at 33-37 East Eighth Street, just a few blocks off Main Street was building in 1915. It cost $50,000.00 and several months to build, employing eleven directors in Jacksonville. There were also eleven directors at the New Rochelle studio.

Edwin Thanhouser, as head of the Thanhouser Company (also referred to as the Thanhouser Film Company) had an illustrious career in a theatre business before starting his film company. He started the Thanhouser Company in October of 1909. He and wife Gertrude owned 99 shares of the capital stock while only 1 share was owned by a brother-in-law and film producer Lloyd F. Lonergran.

Prior to opening the Jacksonville studio the Thanhouser Company had been through some rather extreme changes. Edwin retired from the motion picture business in 1912, selling out to Charles J. Hite and a group of other people. Thanhouser then took his family to Europe on vacation until the outbreak of World War I in 1914. Returning soon after to America, they learned that Charles Hite had died in an auto accident. Subsequently Edwin Thanhouser, at the request of Thanhouser stockholders, returned to head the company he had started. By November of 1915 plans were in the works for a studio in Jacksonville, Florida. . . .

The output of the Jacksonville studio would amount to ten reels per week (as much as any other single producer of the time) on a glass covered stage big enough to hold six movie sets. Kliegl arc lights were used to light scenes on the enclosed stage. Thanhouser made Falstaff comedies, Than-O-Plays (short three reel features) and Thanhouser Mutual Master-Pictures (full length five reel features) in Jacksonville. Our focus, in this book chapter, is solely on the Falstaff comedies.

Figure 8.1. Thanhouser Film Corporation Headquarters, Jacksonville, Florida (Ned Thanhouser Collection).

Some of the staff at Thanhouser included: George A. Grimmer, the studio manager; W. Ray Johnson, the financial auditor; A.H. Moses, chief photographer and technical director; William A. Howell, director of Falstaff brand comedies; Billy Sullivan, co-director of Falstaff comedies; George K. Hollister (formerly with Kalem's Jacksonville studio) was the cameraman for the Falstaff comedies; and William McNulty (also formerly of Kalem studios) was the stage director.

Falstaff comedies were each one-reel in length. The Falstaff name was derived from the character William Shakespeare created. Edwin Thanhouser described these films, in the April 11, 1915 issue of the Morning Telegraph, in the following words...

> I do not want to create the impression that I am trying to compete with or imitate any kind of comedy which is now on the market. I am satisfied to leave the knockabout style of laugh provokers to my confreres. I shall content myself with putting out a very even brand of comedy which will just about keep a continuous smile spread over one's face. Of course it is very likely that I will go further, but I am satisfied to make only modest claims at the beginning, and if the effect of these pictures proves this statement modest I shall certainly be much more content and so will the exhibitors.

Further details were provided in the April 14, 1915 issue of The New York Dramatic Mirror, in which Edwin Thanhouser had this to say...

Hear about Falstaff? That's what's making Friday the big comedy day. Every Friday I am releasing a Falstaff, and you just ask those who used Thanhouser films before I took my vacation whether I ever broke my promise. They'll tell you that you can swear by a film that's got Edwin Thanhouser's guarantee on it. Thanhouser and Falstaff -Quality and Consistency. That's all you need to remember, and your house receipts will never let you forget Thanhouser.

By October 17th, 1915, The Sunday Metropolis paper, in Jacksonville, contributed more details about the new studio...

The selection of Jacksonville as the location for the Thanhouser Film Corporation's Southern studio is largely due to the efforts of the Jacksonville Chamber of Commerce, which has been working to build up this and other industries in this city for some time. The plant, which is to be located on Eighth street just east of Main, will be the only glass moving picture studio in the South and will be thoroughly up to date in every respect, involving an investment of about $30,000 for the studio, open air stage and accessories. From four to five companies will be at work here, employing from 75 to 100 skilled people all the time and numerous others from the city as supernumeraries. The operation of the studio, it is estimated, will cost approximately $1,000 a day.

President Thanhouser of the corporation, while in this city, declared that he had selected Jacksonville in preference to California for the new branch on account of its accessibility to the great Eastern centers. The climate and the fact that pictures can be made out-of-doors the year around, together with the metropolitan advantages of having properties and supplies at hand with little expense, also entered into his decision to establish the plant in Jacksonville.

New Rochelle, N.Y., which is one of the most widely known cities in the world, attributes its fame to the establishment there of a number of moving picture studios and the sending out over the world of photoplays incorporating into their scenes the choicest locations about the city. The Thanhouser Corporation, which makes a number of brands of pictures, all of which are among the most popular in this city, was the first to locate in New Rochelle and is looked upon today as its greatest advertising medium.

Mr. Thanhouser declared while here that the location of other studios in the city had influenced him somewhat in selecting Jacksonville instead of other cities which were seeking his plant, pointing out that the skilled people employed are always much more content where they can have a social set of their own, getting together and discussing each other and people they know in the profession. He believes that the making of pictures in Jacksonville, showing its choicest and most attractive scenes, will prove one of the greatest advantages the city can have in the way of publicity throughout not only this country but all over the civilized world. He also expects other studios to locate in Jacksonville and foresees the time when this city will become the Los Angeles of the Southeast as a moving picture center, pointing out that Los Angeles and many sections of California hold the moving picture industry above all others in value and revenue.

On November 5, 1915 (page 15) yet another article, "Finest Movie Studio in the South to Open in December," further details about the Thanhouser Studio were released to the public.

> Following preliminary work which has been accomplished already, announcement was made yesterday that the finest motion picture studio in the South at least will be that of the Thanhouser Film Corporation on Eight Street, just east of Main Street.
>
> The plant will be ready by early in December and at that time some of the world's greatest stars will be in Jacksonville to act before the cameras of that concern. An expenditure of $35,000 or more is being made in renewing the building and fixing the grounds of the old Rice laundry property which has been secured.
>
> It is stated that when the producing season opens there will be a payroll of upwards of $1,000 per day. . . . Over a month ago Edwin Thanhouser, president of the company, paid a call to Jacksonville and looked over various sites. Mr. Thanhouser states that the climatic conditions here are ideal for a large number of important pictures which he has in the planning .A payroll of seventy-five or so people will be the case here at all times with the studio. . . .

The article "Thanhousers Here to Work At Studio on 8th Street," from page 11 of the December 21, 1915 Florida Times Union, notes "That Everything Will Be in Operation Within Two weeks" and that "President Thanhouser will arrive in City Next Week to Look over Branch." Furthermore. . . .

> The Thanhouser studio, just east of Main on Eighth Street, will be as busy as a beehive within the course of a fortnight, according to a statement of George Grimmer, one of the officials of the corporation, on his arrival in the city yesterday. Following next week. Edwin Thanhouser, president of the company, and Lloyd Lonergan, chief of the scenario department, will arrive. The first work to be done will be five-reel features and one and two-reel comedies, the latter of the famous Falstaff series.
>
> A number of the actors and actresses as well as camera men and technical experts, arrived in the city yesterday on board the Clyde steamer Mohawk. Mr.Grimmer and several officials made the trip here over the Seaboard Air Line railway. Other workers, officials and artists will be reaching the city within the next few days.
>
> The Thanhouser plant here on East Eighth Street will be one of the most complete when it is finished in a few days. Two stages, one of an open air sort and the other of the latest glass and steel construction, will be used. In the old

Rico Laundry building, which was taken over for the use of the studio, a great transformation has been wrought.

"I believe our people will have the most commodious dressing rooms in the country and everything arranged in convenient fashion," stated Mr. Grimmer.

Showing a most accurate knowledge of the minute details of film making, Mrs. Grimmer was the companion of her husband in a trip out to the studio yesterday afternoon. She states that all connected with Thanhouser Corporation are looking forward to the sojourn here with pleasure. . . .

The site of the studio here was personally selected by Edwin Thanhouser, president of the company, in a visit top Jacksonville several months ago. He was taken over the city and suburbs by George E. Leonard. After a consideration of many places he chose the Eighth Street site. The plan of getting ready for actual production work has been hindered by the failure of necessary glass to arrive which is to be used in the covering at one of the studios.

An update on work at the Thanhouser Film Producing was provided by the December 26, 1915 issue of the Florida Times Union newspaper (section1, page 6). In an article titled Thanhousers Are Ready for a Great Season Here in City, there was this account. . . .

That the Thanhouser Film Producing companies are anticipating a great season of activity here was the statement of Edwin Thanhouser, president of the concern, yesterday afternoon He with Lloyd Lonergan are guests of the Hotel Mason and are generally sizing up the motion picture production facilities in Florida. Mr. Lonergan is the scenario director of the corporation and he expects to generally look over the state with a view of using existing conditions in Florida with the themes of several contemplated plays.

Two Thanhouser companies are already in Jacksonville, they being under the direction of Eugene Moore. Feature films are being acted as rapidly as possible at the present. On Friday December 31, George Foster Platt, one of the best known directors of the country, will arrive in Jacksonville with a special company.

In all, the Thanhouser interests contemplate having five companies here who will be extremely busy. . . . Carpenters and technical experts have already arrived in the city. The studio on East Eighth Street is nearing completion, work being held up for some time on account of the failure of certain sorts of construction glass to arrive. . . .

In 1915 the Falstaff brand originated from New Rochelle, and were being released by the Mutual Film Corporation. According to the October 10th issue of New Rochelle's The Morning Telegraph newspaper, in the article "Thanhouser Will Invade Florida" Edwin Thanhouser noted that a Jacksonville, Florida studio would be open for business on December 1st, and that. . . .

The new Jacksonville studio is located near the center of things here, yet it is within easy range of desirable outside locations. It is point of considerable advantage to a manufacturer located in New York. It is a short run there, and I can keep closely in touch with operation without being separated too far from the plant in New Rochelle.... Our responsibility is as great, both to the public and to our own future, as if the printing press had just been invented and we were given control of so large a portion of published matter for the information and entertainment of the millions. This means that we must pay heed to every factor that goes into the making of pictures. It explains why we have enlarged and improved our New Rochelle plant, putting in costly developing, printing, and perforating machinery, a better ventilating system, additional factory space, better studio arrangements, and the like. It is the reason behind the big investment in Jacksonville. It explains why we are holding and continually building up a remarkable organization of actors and directors...All this means also a guarantee to the motion picture public that the Thanhouser product shall at all times be consistently good, always up to a certain high level of merit.

Further details were provided in the December 26th, 1915 issue, section 4, page 14, of Jacksonville's *The Sunday Times-Union* newspaper...

The comedy company is under the direction of William A. Howell, and the principal comedians are Riley Chamberlin, Walter Hiers and Louise Bates... Mr. Howell, comedy director, has been in Jacksonville before, as leading man of a stock company playing here years ago. Walter Hiers, fat boy comedian, has been here three winters, his engagements being with the Majestic and Lubin companies.

In an article from the January 1, 1916 issue of the Florida Times Union (section 4, page 19), in a section called *Thanhouser Topics*, it is stated that. . . .

The quaintest novelty that is yet to hit the moving picture industry is the way the titles of the Thanhouser Falstaff comedies alliterate. If anything could give them the face value of comedies, their titles do that trick. Here are a few of them, which were produced under the direction of William A. Howell, the Falstaff director now in Jacksonville.
   Cousin Clara's Cook Book
   Bing Bang Brothers
   The Soap Sud Stars
   Snowstorm and Sunshine
   Perkins' Peace Party
   Ambitious Awkward Andy
   Maud Miller Modernized
   Theodore's Terrible Thirst

Finger 8.2. Walter Hiers, Thanhouser Company (Ned Thanhouser Collection).

Figure 8.3. Riley Chamberline, Comedian, Thanhouser Company (Ned Thanhouser Collection).

Figure 8.4. Falstaff Comedies, Thanhouser Company (Ned Thanhouser Collection).

Lloyd Lonergan is the man at the Thanhouser studio who devises them, and the public has been quick to catch on. The theater men have taken the opportunity to spring many puns on their audiences because of these titles and in a letter to Mr. Thanhouser one man says 'Long live Lloyd Lonergan's linguistic librettos.

In the January 23, 1916 issue of the Sunday Metropolis (page 5) the completed Jacksonville studio was described, as a *Sunday Metropolis* reporter was given a tour of it...

The city of Jacksonville is to be congratulated on having secured the acquisition in the city of the Thanhouser Film Corporation, one of the largest independent film producers in the United States. The output of the Thanhouser Company, about ten reels per week, is as large as that of any other single producer. A reporter from *The Metropolis*, having received a cordial invitation from Mr. Grimmer, the manager of the local studio, called there recently. Their studio is located at 33 to 37 East Eighth Street, just a few blocks off Main Street. The office was crowded with several dozen extras, waiting in line for the young lady to 'register' them, and Mr. Grimmer was busy interviewing callers, taking care of the wants of the directors and a thousand and one other small matters, while Mr. Johnson, the auditor of finances, was busy signing a huge stack of checks, which will find their way into the offices of Jacksonville merchants and banks.

These gentlemen received the representative cordially and Mr. Johnson volunteered to show him through the large studios and plant.

The interviewer was taken to the enclosed glass covered stage large enough to hold six sets, where Director W. Eugene Moore and the director Leo Wirth were at work on a five-reel Mutual Master-picture...The representative was also introduced to William A Howell, director of the Thanhouser Falstaff brand. He was directing a scene featuring Emerald Bates, the Falstaff Girl, and Walter Hiers, the Thanhouser fat boy. Fatty at the time was playing a chef on board the liner Mohawk, of the Clyde line, where scenes had previously been taken, while the company was enroute from New York to Jacksonville...The reporter was also shown through the company's property rooms, used for the storage of properties and furniture used in the different pictures, and through the electrical department and was shown the working of the large Kliegle arc lights which are used to light scenes taken on the enclosed stage. William McNutty, formerly with the Kalem Company, is the stage director at the Thanhouser studio.

A visit was made to the scenario department where artists were at work painting rocks to look like a cellar wall. Paper hangers were at work here papering sets for pictures to be started soon.

We next visited the carpenter shop, where a group of carpenters were busy on stairs, windows, frames, doors, fireplaces and scenery of all kinds, with William Alexander as head carpenter for the company.

Continuing on to the rear of the glass-covered stage he came to an open court for the parking of the company's autos when not in use. Here also are the dark rooms where the cameramen load their cameras. Next he visited the garage containing two large seven passenger Winston cars and a truck for delivering of props. Carpenters were at work extending the garage to accommodate six cars.

At the rear of the garage is a large open air stage which Mr. Johnson informed us was large enough to accommodate eight large sets. Here we had the pleasure of meeting Director George Foster and his assistant Jason Dunne. We also were delighted to have the opportunity of meeting Miss Doris Grey, the prize beauty of New England, who was selected by the Thanhouser Company from among 39 contestants in a beauty contest...

"Don't go away yet" suggested Mr. Johnson as he was about to leave. "You haven't seen the actors quarters." He was escorted to the second floor of the office building to a spacious green room or lounging room, off of which on all sides open the large dressing rooms. Each room has a window which makes them very light, airy and cheerful, and there is running water on all sides of the building.

Opening off the front of this big green room was a big porch which will greatly add to the comforts of the players in the summertime. "Mr. Grimmer believes in making his players as comfortable as possible," stated Mr. Johnson, "and our studio is just like one big, happy family, working together for the benefit of their pictures."

In a January 30, 1916 issue (section 4, page19) of the *Florida Times Union* the following article appears concerning a Falstaff Chamberlin-Hires comedy. . . .

> William A. Howell is starting this week a new Falstaff comedy that promises to be one of the funniest yet. Riley Chamberlain and Fatty Hires lead in the fun making. It's called Theodore's Terrible Thirst. Riley is Theodore and to cure his 'terrible thirst' they maroon him on a desert island. There are some very funny situations in the play, a great many of the scenes of which are to be taken at Charles S. Hemmenway's estate. In one of the scenes Riley starts to swim off the island only to meet a friendly or perhaps it will be an unfriendly alligator. Mr. Howell is on the lookout for a trained alligator as Riley refuses to do the scene with any amateurs.

In a January 30, 1916(section 4, page 18) issue of the *Florida Times Union*, Thanhouser director W. Eugene Moore expresses his positive feelings about filmmaking in Jacksonville. . . .

> "Jacksonville presents many advantages to the producer of the motion picture," said W.E. Moore to a reporter in the director's office at the Thanhouser plant on Eighth Street. "The photographic value of the light here is far superior to that of Los Angeles. You will notice in photodramas produced in the far West, a peculiar hardness of the shadows; at many times a man's hat will shade and entirely obliterate his eyes and the entire upper portion of his face. This is caused by the lack of moisture in the atmosphere. Moisture diffuses the light and softens the shadows. In California it is sometimes necessary to go directly against photographic rules and face your camera toward the sun to avoid these hard shadows, but here, where the humidity is greater, this disadvantage does not exist, making it possible for us to take all day regardless of the position of the sun. You also offer us a wider variety of scenery than any other place in America. . . . In the North, at this time of the year are troubled with that mysterious quality in photography known as 'static,' which renders film in which it appears practically valueless. Many people advance theories as to the cause of these phenomena, but the experts only know that it exists and is more frequent in cold weather. We find very little trouble with it here."
>
> Mr. Moore is himself a native of the South, hailing from Chesterfield, Va., where he maintains a residence. He has been producing for Thanhouser for the past four years, having been affiliated with Edwin Thanhouser, the president of the company, for the past thirteen years, having directed and played the leading roles in Thanhouser's Stock Company in Milwaukee. His stage career, covering a period of over thirty years, has been an interesting one. . . .

The February 6, 1916 (section 2, page 9) issue of the *Florida Times-Union* newspaper carried a very interesting interview with W. Ray Johnston, described as the auditor of the local Thanhouser Company. The article was titled "Jacksonville Will Become the Hub of Motion Picture Industry says Johnston—If?". . .

"What can the citizens and merchants of Jacksonville do to encourage the motion picture industries to make Jacksonville their home?" asked a Times-Union reporter of Mr. W. Ray Johnston, auditor of finances of the Thanhouser Company one day last week, and here are a few suggestions which he gave.

The city of Jacksonville is fast becoming the Mecca of the East for moving pictures and a few suggestions at this time when your local committee is at work endeavoring to secure some of the biggest companies to make Jacksonville their home might be beneficial.

The moving picture industry, in the short space of a few years, has grown to be the third largest industry in the United States, exceeded only by the oil and automobile industries. There are at the present time 16,000 motion picture theaters in the United States.

"Have you stopped to realize that the motion pictures are but one of a very few industries you could secure for your city which do not take from the natural resources of your country." Mr. Lasky recently made this statement to the board of trade of Los Angeles, and it opened their eyes to the value of the motion picture companies to California.

A box of film is shipped here from New York, is put into a camera, is exposed and is again returned to New York. During the exposing to light of each thousand foot of film about $2 is spent in Jacksonville for each foot of film exposed. This money comes from New York, all sections of the United States and the world into Florida—new working capital for Florida. This money is distributed to the various merchants, hotels, landlords and banks of your city.

It is conservatively estimated that $30,000 outside capital is thus turned loose in Jacksonville each week, when not one cent of the city's resources are taken away.

The people of the city should greet the motion picture manufacturers with open arms and extend to them the use of their grounds and exteriors of their homes for picture purposes. We have found the citizens of Jacksonville very courteous in this respect.

Another matter of considerable importance is the actor, without whom the picture could not be. The merchants of the city should extend to all of these people the usual theatrical discount on purchases made by them. It must be remembered that in New York every store of any consequence allows them this discount and to offer them the advantages of the city of New York, your merchants should do the same. This is done, not only realizing the advertising derived there from, but from the fact that great part of an actor's salary must necessarily be expended on clothes to 'dress their picture.'

A matter also of considerable importance is props. For the settings it is necessary for the manufacturers or producers to call upon your stores to rent them the necessary pieces of settings, such as furniture, curtains, and etc. A great deal of discontent among the manufacturers of California recently was due to overcharge on the rentals of these props. The rental is usually figured on a percentage of the value of the goods, and instances were known where goods valued at $30 were increased to $140 on which to base the percentage charge. This is unfair in the extreme and sure to result in the loss of thousands of dollars to the merchant who uses such methods.

And did you ever think of the advertising value of these pictures taken in Florida and showing Florida's beautiful scenery all over the world.

Allowing for towns whose theaters are closed on Sundays, allowing for the time required to exchange reels at the film exchange and the time the film spends on the road, the feature photoplay runs usually 300 days out of the year. The Jacksonville pictures will be shown for 300 days, let us say twice in the afternoon, and twice in the evening, every twenty-four hours, making a total of 1,200 appearances on the screen yearly. In two years, if this subject survives, its popularity for a full film lifetime. As duplicates of the negative are made and sent all over the United States, Canada, Europe and Australia and South America, it is conservatively estimated that these pictures in total number of appearances will be shown 45,000 times in two years.

Fourteen million people seeing Florida's beautiful country! Can we help but feel at least a small percentage of those will be attracted to visit our state. Does it not behoove the state and its people to encourage the moving picture industry in Jacksonville?

Walter "Fatty" Hiers was born in Cordele, Georgia in 1893, but grew up in Jacksonville and had also lived in Savannah. Prior to Thanhouser, Hires had a brief stage and vaudeville career before working at the Biograph, Lubin, and Majestic film companies. He had always played "country boy" parts.

The Sunday Metropolis (March 14, 1916, page 8) has an interesting story to tell, concerning the Hiers comedy The *Sailor's Smiling Spirit*...

Fatty Hiers, the popular Falstaff comedian, almost took an extended trip abroad last week. We say almost for Fatty did not go abroad but came so near it that there was not fun in it. Director Howell had to take a scene for his Falstaff comedy The Sailor's Smiling Spirit' showing Fatty as a sailor arriving at the docks just in time to catch his boat. They were going to take the scene aboard the Danish barkentine Claudia. While Mr. Howell and his assistant, Billy Sullivan, were figuring out some scheme to get Fatty off the boat after it had started Cameraman Hollister noticed the ship pulling away from the docks and shouted to Fatty to jump aboard, then started to crank. Fatty made a wild jump arriving aboard the rear end of the liner and Billy Sullivan set out in a rowboat, but after getting in midstream it was found impossible to get close enough to the liner to let Fatty off. 'Good-bye, send us a wireless,' shouted Howell and immediately reported to the studio that they had lost their principal comedian. A couple of hours later a telephone call was received from Fatty at Mayport saying that he had been transferred to the tug boat after they reached the mouth of the St. John and that he would return home by train. It is rumored that Hires refuses to do any more comedies calling for sailing steamers.

Riley Chamberlin, Frank McNish and Claude Cooper were three other comedians at the Thanhouser Jacksonville studios. Chamberlin was born November 7th, 1854 in Byron, Michigan, and graduated from Grand Rapids High School in 1854. Subsequently he went on to graduate from Cornell University. He had a 35 year career on the stage before the start of his film career. By 1885 he was back on stage, where he remained for the next quarter century. He played with many prominent actors, including Edwin Booth, appeared in Edwin Thanhouser's stock company, in Milwaukee, and also in Shubert and Frohman productions. By 1911, he was financially secure and ended his stage career. His connection with Edwin Thanhouser's stock company then led to the start, in the spring of 1912, of his movie career. His first comedy film was released in June of that year.

Reel Life noted that "best of everything in the world he (Chamberlin) loves children....They all cling around him, listening to his funny stories, and wherever he moves, the children's laughter follows. Character comedy is Mr. Chamberlin's favorite work in pictures. He puts fun and pathos into his part."

The *New Rochelle Pioneer*, in a November 14, 1914 article by John William Kellette, says of Riley:

> All the glamour of the footlights had vanished when Edwin Thanhouser, who had Riley in stock in Milwaukee, brought him to New Rochelle to pose before the Kleigl lights and the camera, and the applause of the multitudes was missed, but are back in his sub-conscious mind came glints of crowds to urge him on to even better work.

Riley's voice used to be an asset as he trod the boards, and he still retains a singable tone that prevents him being shot when he would chant his muse, but in the silent drama all that is nil and he must depend upon his actions and mannerisms, of which he has many that grants him a pedestal for himself.

> It is not all peaches and cream to do one's best in a three flat side scene, with a director urging on the action, an assistant spotting the footage, and a cameraman cranking a Pathé, and it doesn't help a bit to have the usual onlooker slanting glances one's way and watching scenes where a man of Riley's temperament is booked for such slapstick work as getting kicked in the 18th rib and having his nose tweaked by an irate somebody, nor in being thrown down coal chutes and having coal dumped on one, but to Riley it comes in the game, and he's as willing and ready to be dropped from a roof into a life net, despite his 60 odd years young, to his many unpleasant places that gave Riley Chamberlin the large

following he has. And he's going to retain them. He's an Elk and is in love with New Rochelle. So what more could one ask?

Jacksonville's *Sunday Metropolis* newspaper, on May 14, 1916 (page 5) noted that he is "single, likes girls, is fond of horses and is the self declared 'greatest fisherman the world has ever known.' "In Jacksonville he lived in a rented apartment on Main Street, where he raised pet chickens."

Frank McNish and Claude Cooper starred as the screen characters Oscar and Conrad, in comedies they had previously made at the Thanhouser New Rochelle studio. They were paired by Lloyd F. Lonergan, Thanhouser's scriptwriter. This pair made comedies together from 1916 to 1917. The Oscar and Conrad comedies are listed in the filmography of McNish and Cooper.

McNish was born on December 14, 1853 in Camden, New York. His stage career began around 1870, when he toured in variety acts, and later in New York City at Tony Pastor's 14th Street theatre. Subsequently he toured with McNish, Johnson & Slavin's Minstrels. By 1912 he was appearing, on stage, in Minneapolis, in a vaudeville sketch called *Bonehead Frolics*.

The other half of the Oscar and Conrad comedy team, Claude Hamilton Cooper, was born and educated in London. His first stage appearance at the age of 18 months, at the Royal Theatre in Dublin. At the age of eight his family moved to the United States.

His stage career lasted 21 years, including time in the stock companies of F.F. Proctor, and Charles Dillingham. In 1914 he started his film career at the Thanhouser Company, in New Rochelle. He began appearing in Falstaff comedies in May of 1915.

Prior to that, he worked at Gaumont, as a director at the Solax facility in Fort Lee, New Jersey, and subsequently at Famous Players, All Star, Kinemacolor, Reliance, and Universal.

William A. Howell, director and actor in Falstaff comedies, was born in Cleveland, Ohio in 1877. He was educated at Fordham University, Bronx, New York. Edwin Thanhouser hired him, in August of 1915. Prior to being hired by the Thanhouser Company, Howell had acted on stage in numerous productions and directed stock companies. His screen career also included stints at Rex, Universal, and Majestic studios.

Howell provided an interesting glimpse into his profession, in the January 23, 1916 issue of the *Sunday Metropolis* (page number unknown)...

> Tempo as you know is the prime factor in comedy. We move fast. The day of a slow padded three or more reels comedy is doomed. A story told quickly and humorously in one reel is the only entertainment that I can contribute to the vast program of the Thanhouser branch. I have here everything to bring these comedies to a successful completion—intelligent scenarios, excellent

photography, talented comedians, perfect studios, both artificial lighting and open air, all these, coupled with your glorious sunshine, cooperation of your civic body, business men and householders certainly make my work a pleasure.

Then, I ask you, why shouldn't I enthuse? In fact, since coming to Jacksonville I have taken a new interest in my work. There is no greater restraint to bubbling humor than to have to wait two or three days for fair weather conditions, such as they experience in New York at the present moment.

Your fine enthusiasm dies, so to speak, when you look out from a bleak world. You may be funny to the other fellow, but believe me, you can't possibly see a joke when soaked in the chin with the promise of a fine lunch of pneumonia.

Yes, I know, I have prayed for rain while here, but that was only to allow me to catch up with a couple of hours extra sleep and to get my scenarios in order. Scenarios? Yes, indeed, I have quite a collection—some finished but untrimmed—others in the making, but today I have received the first of comedy scenarios written around locations of Jacksonville and environs. How do I know that my scenarios match up with my locations?

Well, that isn't so difficult. Immediately when I read an accepted scenario I have in my minds eye the location for such a scene. If I am at a loss, there's my photographers to help me in my dilemma.

Thanhouser cameraman George K. Hollister was also, like Howell, very enthusiastic about filmmaking in Jacksonville. In the January 23, 1916 Sunday Metropolis (page 8) he said. . . . "When one takes into consideration that film can be shipped back to New York, be developed and within two days the director has word that all is well or not, and contrast this with a week on the road from Los Angeles...see at a glance what this means to any motion picture company where so much money is spent on production.

Jacksonville is so near New York that it allows those in charge to go freely back and forth and to keep in touch with all the working staff and conditions which spell success.

The great drawback for a permanent studio in Los Angeles at this time is the constant morning fogs that very often do not lift until the better part of the morning has gone, and while it is true that we have rain here, still the heavy rain in that part of the country has often flooded the studios and sites and stopped all operations for days.

That the moving picture people are slowly drifting from their Mecca of Dreams in the land of the Los Angeles may not be that weather conditions alone are the cause, for where nature is gay with her vast mountains, her brooks and streams, and when every nook deems the ideal spot, the manufacturer will spend considerable loss of time, thus paying well for the settings that mean so much to him.

But let us look back to the time when the city held out to the picture makers the golden egg that took them westward. What would they not do to get this vast business located in the city. Well they went, constructed many studios, spent millions and started to work, and now after they are there, what has happened? Graft, it seems, has crept into the hearts of everyone who has a home, or field for sow that these people from the east with all courtesy and willingness to pay for, must use at some time in their pictures.

When I say graft I want to bring into the limelight the seriousness to which same has been practiced upon this business, and when all is written about the exodus from the West, the people will only have themselves to blame, for it has arrived at the point when one can hardly use a porch or gate front without paying five dollars or more. That is graft and the millions of money spent yearly in Los Angeles is slowly drifting back East and South.

With the opportunities that Jacksonville is holding out to the motion picture companies, and with her people the best in the world, and with "Yes, I don't mind if you wish to photograph my home, " and with the smiling face of the director whose path is not always strewn with roses, receiving this help and good will is the very best thing that is denied in the West and this help is going to make Jacksonville the last stop—the home in sunny Florida of thousands of smiling boys and girls who are giving their life work to the movies.

The Moving Picture World, dated April 15, 1916, had the following to say about Falstaff comedies...

It is now about a year since Edwin Thanhouser launched one of his new ideas in the form of the Falstaff brand of comedy. It was at that time announced that these single reelers would represent the direct line of legitimate comedies in vogue. It was pointed out by Mr. Thanhouser that attention would be given first to story; that was the most conspicuous missing element of rapid-fire funny films. The genius of Lloyd Lonergan...was put into play, also Phil Lonergan, his able younger brother...

The original Falstaff director was Arthur Ellery, and his company remained in New Rochelle when it came time to go to Florida. Ellery's grasp of legitimate comedy values makes him easily the most consistent performer in his line, and he gets his results through his very seriousness when he stages the funniest scenes. Frances Keyes is his chief comedy character...Ellery's methods seem to assure positive results, possibly due to his success as a writer of comic short stories. Under the present release schedule the two Falstaffs per week have established their following, but it is expected that new additions will be made to the staff which will put them over with still more vim and smash.

On April 20th, 1916 Jacksonville's *Florida Metropolis* carried an article saying that Riley Chamberlin had left, on the ship Lenape, for New Rochelle—and noted that he expected to return in the fall with others who had already gone back to New Rochelle. This was apparently common practice, to avoid the heat of Jacksonville summers—which presumably made filming more difficult and decreased productivity.

So Thanhouser, and perhaps other film companies with a Jacksonville presence would send most of their company north in the summer, gearing down the Jacksonville presence until the fall -when they could accomplish more.

Chapter Eight

Riley Chamberlin's going back to New Rochelle raised few eyebrows. So too on May 21st when a story in Jacksonville's *The Sunday Times-Union* reported that the studio was closing and even listed the names of the people who were heading North.

In the June 10th, 1916 edition of *The Moving Picture World*, Columnist Carl Louis Gregory confirmed this when he declared...

> There are five companies at the present time operating in Jacksonville: Thanhouser, Eagle, Vim, Kalem, and Gaumont. The weather is beginning to be oppressively warm, and all of the companies except Eagle and Kalem are making preparations to go north for the summer...All of the studios operating here have open-air stages with the exception of the Thanhouser Company, which has a glass studio for rainy days in addition to a large open air studio. The Eagle and Vim studios are the only ones who develop their negatives in Jacksonville, the others sending their stuff north to their respective headquarters for development and printing.

Q. David Bowers, in the 1916 chapter 9 section (of the cd-rom disc he authored) entitled *The Year in Review* mentions that Thanhouser also lost its affiliation with the Mutual organization, and switched to releasing their films through Pathe Exchange, Inc. However, as Bowers notes. . . .

> Nothing was guaranteed. As noted, a review committee was to screen each film and then decide whether Pathé should release it. Gone were the days of one-reel pictures, which had become obsolete anyway, and after midsummer 1916 all Thanhouser Film Corporation films were five reels or more. Falstaff comedies, as each were one-reelers, the closing of the Jacksonville studio aside, had also become obsolete in the more modern film marketplace.
>
> Meanwhile, elsewhere "in the world of comedy, Charlie Chaplin remained dominant and with a contract for $670,000 in his pocket, began what eventually amounted to 12 two-reel films for Mutual. Theatre audiences laughed at the slapstick antics in Keystone comedies, while Harold Lloyd was catching on with his Lonesome Luke pictures produced by Rolin and released through the Pathé Exchange. In the Kalem studio, Lloyd V. Hamilton and Bud Duncan produced the highly successful Ham and Bud series of Mirth provokers. Al Christie, earlier with Nestor, formed Al E. Christie Comedies and began releasing in September 1916, eventually gaining a wide audience.
>
> The old Patents Company members were rapidly fading in the face of aggressive competition by newer studios. Four of them - Kleine, Edison, Selig, and Essanay - banded together in 1916 as K-E-S-E to release their productions, the successor, more or less, to V-L-S-E, formed in April 1915 to distribute Vitagraph, Lubin, Selig, and Essanay films.
>
> By this time the day of the Patents Co. studios vs. the Independents was a subject for the history books.

By December 1916 Edwin Thanhouser was caught up in a high powered industry which bore little resemblance to film production when he began his releases in 1910.

The Greek philosopher Hericlitus once said that "there is nothing permanent except change." In 1916 there were huge changes brewing in the film industy. An article in the December 3, 1916 issue (section 2, page 21) carried the happy news that "the Florida studio of the Thanhouser Film Company out on Eighth Street, will be opened January 1, according to published statements in a New York paper. The article noted that it was "interesting to Jacksonville people who know them and to the Southern assembly of movie artists and manufactures of films in this city, that W. Ray Johnston, who was here with the Thanhouser Company last winter, is now made head of the company's foreign department studio and that he is also the assistant secretary and treasurer of the company.

> The Thanhouser Company has a handsome and complete studio in this city, and those of the company here last winter were among the most popular of the movie folks in the city. The announcement that the studio will open early this season is welcome news to their friends in Jacksonville." By 1917 Edwin Thanhouser had decided to retire. *Variety*, in its September 21, 1917 issue, described the situation...
>
> Edwin Thanhouser is to retire from active participation in the picture field next spring when his present contract with the Thanhouser company expires... The Thanhouser studio at New Rochelle is practically idle now, with no one there except the bookkeeper and Mr. Thanhouser. This condition will in all likelihood prevail until the contract runs out...At present the Thanhouser Company is on clean velvet, not having any liabilities and a bank balance amounting to more than $50,000.

There would be no one returning to Thanhouser's Jacksonville Eighth Street studio to make comedies or any other films.

THANHOUSER COMPANY FILMOGRAPHY

Falstaff Comedies with Walter "Fatty" Hiers...

1916. *The Optimistic Oriental Occults* (January), *Snow Storm and Sunshine* (February), *Perkins' Peace Party* (February), *Theodore's Terrible Thirst* (March), *Ambitious Awkward Andy* (March), *Rupert's Rube Relation* (March), *Paul's Political Pull* (March), *Ruining Randall's Reputation* (April), *The Professor's Peculiar Precautions* (April), *The Sailor's Smiling*

Spirit (April), *Dad's Darling Daughters* (April), *The Kiddies Kaptain Kidd* (May), *Sammy's Semi-Suicide* (May), *Doughnuts* (June)

1917. *When Love Was Blind* (April)

Riley Chamberlin's Falstaff Comedy Appearances...

1912. *Why Tom Signed the Pledge* (June), *Farm and Flat* (June), *Old Dr. Judd* (August), *Now Watch the Professor!* (August), *The Wrecked Taxi* (August), *Conductor 786* (August), *Don't Pinch My Pup* (September), *At the Foot of the Ladder* (September), *Undine* (September), *Please Help the Pore* (September), *A Six-Cylinder Elopement* (October), *Dotty the Dancer* (October), *In a Garden* (October), *Mary's Goat* (October), *A Will and a Way* (December), *Brains vs. Brawn* (December), *The Star of Bethlehem* (December), *A Militant Suffragette* (December).

1913. *While Mrs. McFadden Looked Out* (February), *Some Fools There Were* (February), *His Heroine* (March), *An Honest Young Man* (March), *Her Gallant Knights* (March), *When Ghost Meets Ghost* (April), *Rosie's Revenge* (April), *In Their Hour of Need* (May), *While Baby Slept* (June), *The Top of New York* (July), *Brethren of the Sacred Fish* (July), *The Girl of the Cabaret* (August), *Waiting for Hubby* (August), *Frazzled Finance* (August), *Moths* (Mutual 9-1913), *His Last Bet* (September), *The Official Goat Protector* (September), *The Old Folks at Home* (October), *How Filmy Won His Sweetheart* (October), *The Children's Hour* (November), *The Henpecked Hod Carrier* (November), *What Might Have Been* (December), *The Milkman's Revenge* (December)

1914. *Mrs. Pinkhurst's Proxy* (January), *Two Little Dromios* (January), *Coals of Fire* (January), *The Elevator Man* (January), *Joseph in the Land of Egypt* (February), *The Scientist's Doll* (March), *The Tin Soldier and the Dolls* (4-5-1914), *The Infant Heart Snatcher* (4-19-1914), *The Strategy of Conductor 786* (April), *A Woman's Loyalty* (May), *A Circus Romance* (Princess 5-22-1914), *The Legend of Snow White* (May), *The Scrub Lady* (July), *The Pendulum of Fate* (July), *The Benevolence of Conductor 786* (October), *Mr. Cinderella* (October), *A Messenger of Gladness* (November), *Naidra, the Dream Woman* (December)

1915. *The Dog Catcher's Bride* (January), *Finger Prints of Fate* (January), *The Gratitude of Conductor 786* (February), *The Life Worth Living* (April), *The Actor and the Rube* (April), *Love and Money* (May), *Ferdie Fink's Flirtations* (May), *The Three Roses* (May), *Truly Rural Types* (June), *Ebenezer Explains* (June), *The Stolen Anthurium* (June), *Mme. Blanche, Beauty Doctor* (June), *Tracked Through the Snow* (July), *P. Henry Jenkins and Mars* (July), *Getting the Gardener's Goat* (July), *Help! Help!* (August), *That Poor Damp*

Cow (August), *Biddy Brady's Birthday* (September), *Simon's Swimming Soul Mate* (September), *The Dead Man's Keys* (September), *Con, the Car Conductor* (September), *Cousin Clara's Cook Book* (October), *Capers of College Chaps* (October), *Bing-Bang Brothers* (October), *Tillie, the Terrible Typist* (October), *The Film Favorite's Finish* (November), *Clarence Cheats at Croquet* (December), *The Conductor's Classy Champion* (December), *When William's Whiskers Worked* (December), *Una's Useful Uncle* (December).

1916. *The Optimistic Oriental Occults* (January), *Grace's Gorgeous Gowns* (January), *Pete's Persian Princess* (January), *Lucky Larry's Lady Love* (January), *Snow Storm and Sunshine* (February), *Perkins' Peace Party* (February), *Maud Muller Modernized* (March), *Ambitious Awkward Andy* (March), *Theodore's Terrible Thirst* (Marchj), *Rupert's Rube Relation* (March), *Paul's Political Pull* (March), *Ruining Randall's Reputation* (April), *The Professor's Peculiar Precautions* (April), *The Sailor's Smiling Spirit* (April), *Dad's Darling Daughters* (April), *The Kiddie's Kaptain Kidd* (May), *Politickers* (May), *Disguisers* (May), *Making the Major a Mayor* (Falstaff 6-15-1916; ready for release but not issued), *Doughnuts* (June), *Fare, Lady* (August), *In Mexico* (August), *Prudence the Pirate* (October)

1917. *Her New York* (January)

Frank McNish Falstaff Comedy Appearances...

1915. *The Postmaster of Pineapple Plains* (November), *The Conductor's Classy Champion* (December)

1916. *The Optimistic Oriental Occults* (January), *Booming the Boxing Business* (February), *Silas Marner* (February), *Rustie Reggie's Record* (February), *Oscar, the Oyster Opener* (March), *Theodore's Terrible Thirst* (March), *Rupert's Rube Relation* (March), *Sapville's Stalwart Son* (April), *The Overworked Oversea Overseer* (April), *Simple Simon's Schooling* (April), *The Skilful Sleigher's Strategy* (May), *Deteckters* (May), *Politickers* (May), *Disguisers* (May), *Advertisementers* (June), *Real Estaters* (June), *Romeoers* (June, ready but not issued), *Guiders* (August), *Musickers* (September).

Falstaff Comedy appearances of Claude Cooper...

1914. *A Debut in the Secret Service* (April), *The Strike* (April)

1915. *The Stolen Jewels* (March), *A Freight Car Honeymoon* (June), *The Country Girl* (June), *The Silent Co-Ed* (July), *The Picture of Dorian Gray* (July), *P. Henry Jenkins and Mars* (July), *Pansy's Prison Pies* (August), *Weighed in the Balance* (August), *When Hungry Hamlet Fled* (August),

Bessie's Bachelor Boobs (September), *Gustav Gebhardt's Gutter Band* (September), *A Perplexing Pickle Puzzle* (September), *Busted But Benevolent* (October), *Hattie, the Hair Heiress* (October), *"Clarissa's" Charming Calf* (November), *Lulu's Lost Lotharios* (November), *A Cunning Canal-Boat Cupid* (November), *Minnie, the Mean Manicurist* (December), *Bill Bunks the Bandits* (December).

1916. *Hilda's Husky Helper* (January), *Grace's Gorgeous Gowns* (January), *Pete's Persian Princess* (January), *Booming the Boxing Business* (February), *Rustie Reggie's Record* (February), *Oscar, the Oyster Opener* (February), *Sapville's Stalwart Son* (April), *The Overworked Oversea Overseer* (April), *Simple Simon's Schooling* (April), *Deteckters* (May), *Politickers* (May), *Disguisers* (May), *Advertisementers* (June), *Real Estaters* (June), *Romeoers* (June; ready for release but not issued), *Making the Major a Mayor* (June; ready for release but not issued), *Guiders* (August), *Musickers* (September).

1917. *The Woman in White* (July).

Oscar and Conrad Comedies

Rusty Reggie's Record (February), Oscar, the Oyster Opener (March), Sapville's Stalwart Son (April), The Overworked Oversea Overseer (April), Simple Simon's Schooling (April), Deteckters (May), Politickers (May), Disguisers (May), Advertisementers (June), Real Estaters (June), Romeoers (June, ready but not issued), Making the Major a Mayor (June, ready for release but not issued), Guiders (August), Musickers (September).

William A. Howell directed Falstaff Comedies ...

1915. *Cousin Clara's Cook Book* (October), *Freddie, the Fake Fisherwoman* (November), *Hannah's Hen-Pecked Husband* (November).

1916. *The Optimistic Oriental Occults* (January), *Snow Storm and Sunshine* (February), *Perkins' Peace Party* (February), *Maud Muller Modernized* (March), *Ambitious Awkward Andy* (March), *Theodore's Terrible Thirst* (March), *Rupert's Rube Relation* (March), *Paul's Political Pull* (March), *Ruining Randall's Reputation* (April), *The Professor's Peculiar Precautions* (April), *The Sailor's Smiling Spirit* (April), *Dad's Darling Daughters* (April), *The Kiddies' Kaptain Kidd* (May), *Sammy's Semi-Suicide* (May), *Doughnuts* (June).

Chapter Nine

Klever Pictures, Inc.

Klever Pictures, Inc. located at 32 East Main Street made Klever Komedies between late 1916 and late 1919. Victor Moore was Executive Officer and R.R. Riskin was business manager.

The book American Silent Film Comedies, by this author, says that Victor Moore's Klever Komedies were made by Jesse L. Lasky Feature Play Company made for release through Paramount Pictures Corporation. The Lasky Company had offices at 120 West 41st Street in New York City. In total the company made over fifty one-reel comedies starring Victor Moore, which were directed by Harry Jackson.

Moore came to Klever from a background in comedy roles on both the vaudeville and Broadway stages. He had also acted in the films *Chimmie Fadden*, and *Chimmie Faden Out West*—both directed by Cecil B. Demille in 1915 and financed by Jesse Lasky Feature Play Company. In 1916 the Jesse Lasky Feature Play Company merged with Adolph Zukor's Famous Players. In 1927.they joined Paramount Pictures.

Arriving in Jacksonville, in December of 1916, the first comedy was completed that month. It was titled *The Best Man*. Others included: *Bungalowing* (June 1917), *Commuting* (June 1917), *Moving* (March 1917) and *Flivvering* (March 1917).

The trade publication *Motography*, for December 2, 1916 (Volume 16, Number 23, page 1240) reported on the activities of Klever Pictures, Inc. in the following article. . . .

> Paramount Picture Corporation will release exclusively in connection with its other 'little features.' The productions of Klever Pictures, Inc., known as Klever Komedies, in which Victor Moore, the well-known comedian, will be starred. These comedies will be released bi-weekly, alternating with the single reel

Black Diamond comedies which have been distributed by Paramount during the last two months. Victor Moore has been interested in single-reel comedies for the past two years.

When he obtained his release a few months ago from the Lasky Feature Play Company, in whose productions he had appeared for Paramount, he immediately set out to organize a company to produce single-reel comedies, and his affiliations were naturally with those concerns that were then negotiating to release through Paramount.

The addition of the Klever Komedies to the exhibitors' program released by Paramount, now rounds out their service in a most excellent manner, as they are already releasing in connection with their four, five and six-reel features, produced by Famous Players Film Company, the Jesse L. Lasky Feature Play Company, the Oliver Morosco Photoplay Company and Pallus Pictures, three single-reel features each week , the Paramount Pictographs, the magazine-on-the-screen , the Paramount Burton Holmes Travel Pictures, and the Paramount-Bray Cartoons.

The first release, 'The Best Man,' will be given to the public on December 4, and will be followed every two weeks by a new subject. Mr. Moore has surrounded himself with an excellent cast of legitimate comedy players and will be assisted in the direction of these comedies by Harry Jackson.

The officials of Paramount have gone to every extreme to obtain a class of comedies that blend with the quality of their features and weave themselves properly into the exhibitor's regular program scheme, and which would attractively add to the type of better pictures for better theaters and a better public, upon which foundation Paramount has built since its inception.

Jacksonville's *Florida Metropolis* newspaper reported on December 3, 1916 (page 2) that "Victor Moore, with a large company of Klever Picture Players, will arrive at the Garrick Studios Monday for the winter. Mr. Moore is producing comedies of the first water, and his arrival in the city will be welcomed."

Additional information about the Klever Company was provided by the December 16, 1916 (page 6) *Florida Metropolis*—in an article entitled "Klever Picture Players Pleased with Jax Spirit: Large Company Making One-Reel Victor Moore Comedies at the Garrick Studios..."

> We can't understand why this city should not become the greatest motion picture producing center in the United States , declared one of the members of the Klever Pictures Company,' as we have never found hospitality extended to members of the silent drama as it has been here, and with such a gracious hand. We have found the municipal authorities in both Jacksonville and South Jacksonville ready to cooperate with us in every way, and the citizens, with whom we must, of course, come in closer touch, have extended to us the glad hand of friendship, which surely no member of the profession would violate.

Figure 9.1. Victor Moore, Principal Comedian, Klever Komedies (Blair Miller Collection). Credit: Wisconsin Center for Film and Theater Research.

R. Robert Blakin of the Klever players declares that he does not understand why big producers will send companies on a four or five-day journey to the Pacific coast, during which they must lose a great deal of valuable time en route, when Jacksonville is only twenty-seven hours from Broadway by rail, and the steamship lines offer such opportunities to make pictures if a company is sent by this route.

Practically the entire personnel of the Klever picture players are registered at the Hotel Mason, where they will remain during the winter. Those in the company are Victor Moore, Emma Littlefield, Michael Oven Bach, Alex Oven Bach, Maurice Elliott, Helen Sallinger, Harry Jackson, Grace Stevens, Saryl Fleming, Frank Pernglik, Robert Riskin, Bradley Martin, Albert Rinn, Jesse Courtney, H. Semole, Edward McWage and J.R. McCaffry.'"

By December 25, 1916 (page 5) the *Florida Metropolis* was noting progress at Klever... "The new main stage of the Victor Moore Company, of Klever players on East Ninth Street, is completed, and the first scene taken Friday. The company have their offices, dressing rooms, and workshop and, in fact, complete studio located in a three-story building adjoining the Thanhouser studio."

The *Moving Picture World* of June 30, 1917 (Volume 32, #13, page 2125) contained an article "Moore to Increase His Klever Komedies," in which the following information is given. . . .

Victor Moore, the well known comedian, has returned to New York, from his motion picture studio in Jacksonville, Fla., to establish another studio in the metropolis, and to make his plans for the producing of his future single reel Klever Komedies, which are released by Paramount Pictures Corporation to all exhibitors.

It has taken Mr. Moore, who was a favorite in five reel comedies, having starred in some of the most successful Lasky productions, less than six months to realize that the greatest demand in the motion picture industry today from the exhibitor's standpoint is feature single reel pictures. When he originally entered the short feature field, with the sole intention of raising the standard of single reel comedies . . . he has not only proved that single reel comedies are not 'fillers' but are actually 'added attractions' to the five or six reelers on the bill, are what the exhibitors want and is now planning to erect a second studio and to increase his output by 100 per cent.

Mr. Moore will add another director to his staff and is also picking a number of new players to appear in support with him in his future pictures. Thomas J. Grey has also been added to the scenario department and is now preparing a number of clever scripts which Mr. Moore will produce in his new studio this summer.

"My one ambition is to make one reel features," said Mr. Moore in speaking of his new plans, 'and to that end I am enlarging my producing, executive and scenario departments. It is perfectly natural for everyone to prefer to make and appear in five or six reel features, but when you look over the field from the exhibitor's standpoint, and analyze the situation you will find that the greatest need today is the single reel feature.

"I have studied the proposition carefully, and I know that it is one best bet for the exhibitor, and I have but one ambition and that is to give them this material. My additional studio will be equipped with the best of everything."

An additional member, Peggy Adams, joined the cast around October of 1917, according to the October 13, 1917 (page 219) issue of *The Moving Picture World*. Adams was to be Victor Moore's new leading lady. The article notes that Chester DeVonde is now director, a change from Harry Jackson who was initially credited as director. Devonde chose Adams "to play the lead in but one Victor Moore comedy, but her one week has extended into several and now she is a permanent feature with the Klever Komedy organization. Miss Adams is a beautiful young brunette, with heaps of excellent experience. Her home is in Toronto and most of her professional work has been on the Coast. Her understanding of comedy is enhanced by a dash and daring which makes her an admirable coworker for Mr. Moore."

America entered World War I on April 6, 1917. Klever Komedies mirrored the concerns of many Americans in the scenarios of these comedies. Steven R. Webb, writing in *Film History* magazine[1] noted that "...the Klever Komedies were aimed at the realities and absurdities that the war created in the day-to-day lives of those on the home front. As such they seemed to find an appreciative audience...The films move from no mention of the war at all in the early part of the year (1917), to a brief recognition of the soldier as hero image at the war's outset, to a latency period during the initial months of America's involvement in the war, to a flurry of activity as effects of the war began to become facts of life. Thus, at least one studio, as the war moved on, its intrusion on and importance in the daily life of Americans became too compelling to ignore."

NOTE

1. *Film History* magazine, page 111, 1989, Volume 3.

Chapter Ten

Klutho Studios

Klutho Sudios was located at 22 West Ninth Street, between Main and Laura Streets. Klutho's president was H.J. Klutho; vice-president, Fay Smith; secretary, Harland Smith; general manager, Virgil MacKenzie; and directors, Glen Lambert and Bert Tracy.

According to the book *Jacksonville's Architectural Heritage: Landmarks for the Future*, Klutho "had been practicing on his own for two years in New York when in 1901 he read about the devastating fire in Jacksonville. Within a month he moved to this city to join in its reconstruction. . . ." He came to Jacksonville from New York City, where he'd studied design and practice of architecture, in the aftermath of the Great Fire. In the aftermath of the Great Fire, his designs were used in many of Jacksonville's buildings and he became Jacksonville's leading architect.

A Jacksonville architect, Henry John Klutho spent $40,000.00 to build the studio, which included an indoor stage 60 x 60 feet, and an outdoor filming area 48 x 144 feet.[1] While construction began in 1916, it was not completed until 1917—when the exodus of studios leaving Jacksonville was beginning.[2] It was the last studio to open in Jacksonville. Electrical equipment came from the defunct Kalem studios, which went out of business in 1915, when Klutho was just getting started in the movie business. Kalem's film output had concentrated exclusively on one-reel films and could not compete once longer two-reel and feature length films were marketed.

Klutho also rented studio space to Yorke-Metro studios, Paramount, Florida Funny Film Corporation, and the Briggs Comedy Pictures, Inc.

- Paramount made a series of "Regular Fellow" comedies, which were similar to Hal Roach's "Our Gang" comedies. Victor Moore made some of his Paramount comedies at the Klutho studios.

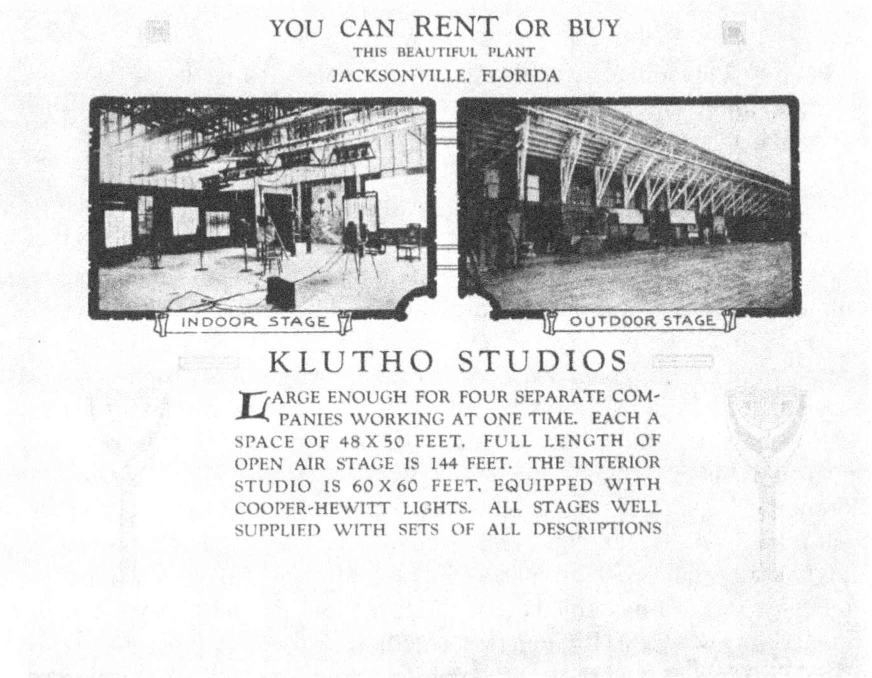

Figure 10.1. Klutho Studios—Interior and Exterior Stages (Blair Miller Collection).

Figure 10.2. Klutho Studios—Interior Stage (Blair Miller Collection).

- "Funny" Fatty Filbert was the star of the comedies made by the Florida Funny Film Corporation.
- The manager at the Briggs Comedy Pictures, Inc was Alex Yokel.

The Florida Motion Picture Company also had a connection with the Klutho studios. According to the Motion Picture Studio Directory and Trade Annual[3], a Florida Motion Picture Corporation made Sunbeam Comedies (other sources call these Sunshine Comedies) at the Klutho studios. These comedies starred Hilliard "Fatty" Carr (sometimes spelled Karr) and were made at the Klutho studios until about 1922. Also called the Hamilton Photoplay Company, this company made low budget rube comedies starring and written by Pearl Gaddis, and filmed on the streets of Jacksonville. They were directed by Glen Lambert, who subsequently worked for the United States Film Corporation. Lambert's experience in the film world also included stints at Metro-Goldwyn-Mayer, 20th Century-Fox, Universal, Hal Roach, Mack Sennett, Crystal Studios in New York, Biograph Studio, Vim Studio, Lubin Film Company, Pete Smith comedies, Walt Disney Studio and his own studio, in Miami, Florida, Miami Lightening Comedies.

In 1971 Glen Lambert was interviewed by Ron Sercombe, a Florida Times Union staff writer.("When Flicks Flickered Here," *Florida Times Union*, January 17,1971, pages 1-8) In the interview Lambert recalled his extensive background in the film business and in particular his time at Klutho studios. The article notes that. . . .

> For about four years Jacksonville was a motion picture center. Actually threatening the prestige of Hollywood. At least a hundred films—most of them two-reelers and the majority of them comedies—were produced in Jacksonville. . . .
>
> Lambert started producing 'Sunbeam Comedies' for Klutho . . . Lambert, between films, made up 'location views' and took them to Hollywood where they were viewed by many of the top studio heads.
>
> "They were interested," Lambert said. "So interested that at least a half dozen Hollywood studio executives came to Jacksonville." They were tremendously impressed with the weather conditions in Jacksonville. On an average, there are 227 days out of 360 a year when exterior motion pictures can be shot most of the time. That's a great improvement over Los Angeles with its perpetual smog and recurring fog.
>
> Only trouble was the studio wasn't large enough for the stupendous, horrendous, hilarious, unforgettable type of films that were coming into vogue about that time and no one in Hollywood—or in Jacksonville—was willing to put up enough money for a really adequate studio. . . .

There is also some evidence indicating that Paramount and Metro studios filmed here. Perhaps Paramount Victor Moore comedies were made at Klutho, but this cannot be verified by my research.

In 1920 the Klutho studio was sold to Berg Productions, where Billy West was to make a comeback. Details of the sale were provided in the July 28, 1920 (Section 2, front page) issue of the *Florida Times Union* newspaper, in an article titled New York Movie Co. Buys Klutho Filming Studio. . . .

> Berg Productions, moving picture producing company of New York, yesterday purchased the Klutho studios in this city, the consideration being in the neighborhood of $60,000, according to H.T. Berg, general manager of the company, who closed the deal here. Arthur Kimball, banker of New York, is president of the Berg Productions, Mr. Berg stated.
>
> The Berg Productions have three producing companies. They are Screen Craft, Julie Elvidge the star, Billy West comedies. Billy West the star, and Special Productions, producers of seven-reel features. The Billy West Comedies Company will arrive here in about a week and begin work, Mr. Berg said yesterday. The Berg Productions will establish a complete scenario department here.
>
> Victor Kremer has a lease on part of the Klutho studios for a period of four months, and will occupy with the Berg companies for that time. The Kremer Company expects to begin work here about August 15.
>
> Mr. Berg left last evening for Savannah where he is to meet June Elvidge. Following his conference in Savannah he planned to go to California. One of the Berg companies is now operating in that state.

Victor Kremer is identified, in the book *American Silent Film Comedies: An Illustrated Encyclopedia of Persons, Studios and Terminology*, by Blair Miller, as having bought the prints and negatives of the Essanay Film Manufacturing Company in 1919. Subsequently he made them available for reissue. Essanay stopped producing films in 1918. The studio closed in 1922.[4]

NOTES

1. Craig Florida Times-Union article and Nelson (page 527).
2. Nelson, page 527.
3. Published in 1920 by the Motion Picture News, Inc., 729 Seventh Avenue in New York City. Also published in Chicago and Los Angeles. Richard Alan Nelson, in his *Florida and the American Motion Picture Industry,* 1898-1930 (UMI reprint, 1997), pages 519, 527, and 529 also notes these were Sunbeam Comedies.
4. Nelson, page 527.

Chapter Eleven

Other Studios

A number of movie studios were established only briefly (compared to studios such as Vim, Thanhouser or the others we have detailed in this book) in Jacksonville.

One such studio was the Encore Pictures Corporation, which was started by Harry Myers and Fernando "Tweedledum" Perez in the aftermath of the Vim Comedy Company closing their studio. They initially had assets of $30,000.00 in stocks and capitalization of $50,000.00 when they started the company. They produced in Jacksonville until the end of World War I.

Relatively little is known about most of these companies. The Majestic-Punch Comedy Company established their studio at the Ostrich farm in Jacksonville. Until April of 1913 Jerry Gill was the lead actress—thereafter she was replaced by Laura Lyman. Gill left the company to return to New York City.

According to the book *Jacksonville after the Fire*, 1901-1919: A New South City, page 105, footnote 18, The Ostrich Farm was "Jacksonville's first amusement park" and "located out Talleyrand Avenue in the Fairfield section east of downtown. It opened in the winter of 1898-99. Initially visitors, mostly tourists, could watch ostriches race, ride in ostrich-drawn carts, or even saddle up one of the big birds."

Seeking to compete with Dixieland Park amusement center, racing ostriches Oliver W. Oliver Jr. and Cyclone, and other attractions, were added. The Ostrich Farm moved, and the reopened at Phoenix Park in 1901, but was now called the Florida Ostrich and Alligator Farm. A cornucopia of attractions grew to include, by 1907, a polar bear alligators, baby lions, pumas, leopards, sloths, monkeys, birds, and other jungle animals, lion wrestling, balloons ascending with parachute jumps, performing stallions, comedy acrobats, high-wire acts, free vaudeville, roller coasters, merry-go-rounds, a

Figure 11.1. Dixieland Theatre, Dixieland Park, Jacksonville, Florida (Florida Collection, Jacksonville Public Library).

Figure 11.2. Café and Dancing Pavilion, Dixieland Park, Jacksonville, Florida (Florida Collection, Jacksonville Public Library).

Figure 11.3. Dixieland Park, Jacksonville, Florida (Florida Collection, Jacksonville Public Library).

Figure 11.4. Entrance to Ostrich Farm, Jacksonville, Florida (Florida Collection, Jacksonville Public Library).

Figure 11.5. Ostrich Farm, Jacksonville, Florida (Florida Collection, Jacksonville Public Library).

Figure 11.6. At the Ostrich Farm, Jacksonville, Florida (Blair Miller Collection).

dance hall, bathing beach, ice cream parlor band concerts, and other attractions too numerous to mention. In Jacksonville After the Fire, it is noted that "tickets cost ten cents, later increasing to twenty-five cents per person." At some point it became known simply as the Ostrich Farm and Zoo.

Dixieland Park opened March 9, 1907 on the riverfront in South Jacksonville. The Park Theater, as part of the Dixieland Park complex, was where major studios rented space to make films. Amber Star Company, in the aftermath of the Vim Company breakup, was located, for awhile, at Dixieland Park (see Amber Star Company & the Eastern Film Company chapter.) Filming in Jacksonville, at Park Theater on a more limited basis were: The Selig Polyscope Company and Essanay Companies both made westerns and animal pictures here. The Selig Company made Tom Mix western films here. The Edison Company made religious films here and Thomas Edison himself frequently visited his studio here when wintering in Fort Myers. Gaumont, Vitagraph, and Biograph studios also made movies at Park Theater on a limited basis.

The book *Jacksonville After the Fire* (page 106, footnote 19) notes the following details regarding Dixieland. . . .

> In 1907 Dixieland Amusement Park opened across the St. Johns River in South Jacksonville, a ferryboat ride from downtown. The Times-Union called Dixieland "The Coney Island of the South." The park contained thirty acres with 100,000 feet of river frontage. In addition to a 1,600-seat theater, there was a Figure-Eight ride, toboggan, merry-go-round, dance pavilion, electric fountain, curio shop, swimming area in the St. Johns River (and later a hundred-foot pool), commons for baseball or circus (and later a ballpark for the Jacksonville Sally League team), refreshment pavilion, dog and pony show, photographic gallery, laughing gallery, circle swing "House of Troubles," botanical garden, and animal life exhibit. A major fire destroyed a large segment of Dixieland in 1909, it was rebuilt but suffered another fire a year later; and finally was closed. . . .

James Craig, in the *Florida Times-Union* article of May 29, 1949 entitled Jacksonville Once Winter 'Film Capital' of World; Kalem came Here in 1907, notes that "famous persons, both in business and the film world, were frequent visitors in Jacksonville during the days of motion picture activity here." Though time has obscured a complete tally of these people, reference was found to several.

Keystone Comedy Company, represented by Adam Kessel and Mabel Normand, visited Jacksonville in 1916—but never actually opened a studio.[1] Details of this trip are provided by an article in the January 30, 1916 issue of the *Florida Times-Union* newspaper (section 4, page 19) in an article titled Keystone Company May Locate Here at Early Date. The text of the article provides the following details. . . .

A. Kessel, Jr., president of the Keystone Film Company of New York, was in Jacksonville Thursday, and it is understood it will return within two weeks with a company of players headed by Mabel Normand, who will work here for the remainder of the winter season. It was learned from good authority that six of the Keystone Company's men would be here this week for the purpose of locating and closing up for a motion picture studio in Jacksonville. This company makes the excellent pictures which are now being shown at the Prince Theater, and if they should decide to locate in Jacksonville they will receive a most cordial welcome.

Gaumont Studios, under the leadership of Richard Garrick, was another studio that called the Dixieland Park Theater home. According to the book Old Hickory's Town (page 193), Richard Garrick was initially affiliated with French Company called Gaumont Players. . . .

When Gaumont Players, a French company with studios in Dixieland Park, left in June 1916, Richard Garrick resigned from the firm and formed Garrick Studios Company. A month later he announced plans to build a rental studio complex. It would be as large as Universal City in Los Angeles. He said the facility would have accommodations for 20 companies, a film-processing lab, carpentry shops, dressing rooms and a restaurant.

Further details were provided in an article in the *Florida Times-Union* newspaper. On July 5, 1916 (section 2, page 11 w) the article is entitled "Garrick Studio Is Start for Jacksonville to Elipse the Los Angeles Picture Colony. . . ."

Announcement in yesterday's *Florida Times-Union* by Richard Garrick, the well known motion picture producer and director, that work will commence here in two weeks for erection of the second largest general studio in America has resulted in commendatory expressions and much speculation as to the ultimate possibilities for the studio eclipsing even the famous Universal City, which from the beginning will be its only peer.

The advantageous geographic location of Jacksonville over that of Los Angeles and other points along the Pacific coast, the time saved in travel by companies that come to Florida for producing purposes instead of going West and the enormous monthly and yearly payroll surrendered by actors and other individuals connected with the industry by the city of Los Angeles alone furnished dome food for favorable reflection.

Since early last winter when so many producing companies began coming to Florida for brief stays and the plan was first conceived to make Jacksonville the principal city on the Atlantic coast for producing, there have been numerous announcements or bold suggestions about this interest and those making arrangements to purchase property here and develop large studios facilities. While some of this talk may have been forthcoming from the best intentions and sincere purpose, other instances have plainly shown that such announcements could be handed out to the public for more advertising purposes of many kinds, with no intention of following them up with tangible results.

Now Mr. Garrick has returned with everything arranged quietly beforehand to begin building not only a studio for motion picture making but a studio that is to surpass anything to be found anywhere else in America except Universal City, those public spirited citizens of Jacksonville who have held on to a stolid faith in possibilities for the picture industry here are voicing their approval in the loudest terms and subsequently speculating into the future. . . . From the moment the great $160,000 plant is started money is going to be paid out here for building materials, workmen and supplies. Then, when it is ready for use by tenant companies the actors and attaches of the director's staffs will be another source of money for Jacksonville business houses.

The capacity of the studio will be for twenty companies, each averaging ten principals and about one hundred supers. With every available portion of rental space taken and the full number of companies operating a minimum of between 2,200 and 2,500 persons would be here, and every one of them spending parts of their salary in Jacksonville. . . . Mr. Garrick last night declared that he had received a large number of congratulations from Jacksonville people upon his development of this corporation and that he felt gratified over the hearty cooperation shown him and his associates from the start. Other business men of the city expressed their approval and pleasure otherwise, watch in a like manner reflected the general sentiment that the new studio is the actual beginning of Jacksonville's entry into the production field as a formidable competitor of Los Angeles.

"I think that the building of this studio here will mean a great deal of good for the city," said J.J. Heard of the Heard National Bank. "It will bring many new people here and greatly facilitate the motion picture interests in their work."

From the point of view of the hotel man . . . Manager Charles G. Day, of the Hotel Seminole, declared that, with the studio in operation as a natural stimulus to promoting the industry here, he believes every line of business will be benefited.

"First of all, I am pleased that this studio is to be managed and directed by Richard Gerick," he said. "Having met a great many of the producers and directors through the hotel business and having come to know them intimately, I have always admired Mr. Garrick, because he combined in his make-up the experienced director and producer with keen business knowledge.

I believe that other business men here realize this excellent combination and regard him as a man best fitted to build and direct such a project. During his stay here last winter, his popularity with men of affairs was unequalled by any, and I am glad that he is here to become one of us and to bring us such a big industry.

Second, my experience with the motion picture people is that they are the most liberal people in the world, when they have money to spend. The accumulation of a large colony of them throughout the year, as this studio will ultimately do, will bring thousands and thousands of dollars to the Jacksonville merchants and create a year-round industry for us."

Elsie MacLeod was the leading comedienne and director at the United States Film Corporation. Her prior film experience included stints at the Edison, Kalem, Vim and Fox studios. In an October 8, 1916 advertisement, in the *Florida Times-Union*, (section 2, page 22) the following information appears. . . .

> The United States Film Corporation (Incorporated Under the Laws of Florida) Now Offer First and Foremost to Florida Capital Stock at Par Value. $10.00 per Share. Only a limited number of shares can be had at this price. This gives you an opportunity of getting in on the ground floor in what we consider will develop into the greatest moving picture proposition in the south. "Great Oaks from Little Acorns Grow."
>
> We are starting with a capitalization of only $15,000 and indications point to great success in this field. We have already secured our location at very nominal cost. Experience has taught is that it does not require a $100,000 studio to produce the best pictures.
>
> If you have a little money to invest, we know of nothing that will give you better returns than the Motion Picture Business. Further information will be cheerfully given on request.
>
> Call, write or phone us. United States Film Corporation. 401 Duval Bldg. Jacksonville, Fla. Invest Your Money at Home.

The Black Diamond studios, according to the Motion Picture Studio Directory and Trade Annual (see previous footnote for same), had a studio on Tallyrand Avenue. This is the same studio mentioned in *American Silent Film Comedies*[2], by Blair Miller, as having been in Wilkes-Barre, Pennsylvania.

Cuckoo Comedies, on Riverside Avenue in Jacksonville, was owned by Mark Dintenfass—former partner in the Vim Comedy Company. Will Lewis, Jr. was the studio manager.[3]

NOTES

1. Florida Times-Union, Craig article, May 29, 1949 (page 12) and June 5, 1949 (page 21).
2. *American Silent Film Comedies: An Illustrated Encyclopedia of Persons, Studios and Terminology,* McFarland & Company, Inc., 1995.
3. As mentioned in the Motion Picture Studio Directory and Trade Annual, 1920, page number unknown.

Chapter Twelve

What Happened to the Dream of Making Jacksonville into What Hollywood, California Ultimately Became?

A myriad of reasons seem to account for Jacksonville never having become the center of the motion picture business that Hollywood became. For each movie company these reasons would seem to be different—yet taken as a whole they are a reflection of the state of the world in which they were doing business.

World War I disrupted many of the established routes for marketing films to the European countries, and so limited the potential for a number of film companies. America entered the "war to end all wars" on April 6, 1917. Richard Garrick's studios, at Dixieland's Park Theater, was first aligned with Gaumont Players, a French company. When Gaumont left Jacksonville, in June 1916, it was due to the gathering clouds of war, and uncertainty about the future. They returned to France, Richard Garrick formed Garrick Studios Company, and continued to make films. Garrick Studios was home to the film companies Amber Star, Edison, Essanay, Selig Polyscope and others. Garrick essentially would rent studio space to other studios at the Park Theater and presumably rent them equipment too, if needed.

Kalem was the first to locate in Jacksonville and the first to go out of business. They closed the Jacksonville studio in 1917, after trying unsuccessfully to merge their Jacksonville and Santa Monica, California studios, in California. Rose Melville retired, with her husband Frank Minzey, to her home at Lake George, N.Y.—built largely from the vaudeville success of Sis Hopkins.

Lubin closed the Jacksonville studio on February 13, 1915. In 1916 Lubin merged with Vitagraph, Selig and Essanay (in a deal engineered by Benjamin B Hampton) to become the Greater Vitagraph studios. (For more details see the book American Silent Film Comedies, by this author.)

Vim Comedy Company, on the other hand, was saddled with poor management. The disputes over finances would ultimately doom the Vim enterprises—but lead to the creation of both Amber Star Comedies, which became Jaxon Comedies, and the King-Bee Films Corporation. Amber Star moved to Providence, Rhode Island. King-Bee left Jacksonville, filmed briefly in New York City, then moved to 1329 Gordon Street. Los Angeles, California.

Eagle was one of only three studios still operating in Jacksonville at the end of World War I. Eagle's main comic, Fernando Perez, or Tweedledum (as he was known in the films he made for Eagle in 1916) would go on to work at Vim—where he became known as the film character Bungles. Later, in 1918, he appeared as Twede-Dan in a series made by the Jester Film Company.

As for the Thanhouser Company, it seems a combination of the retirement of Edwin Thanhouser, and a changing industry, caused their demise. One-reel comedies (such as their Falstaff brand) became archaic in the face of the longer multi-reel comedies such as what Charlie Chaplin was making for the Mutual Film Corporation.

It is unknown specifically, by my research, what happened to Klever Pictures Company—except to say that it was making one-reel comedies and they went the way of the dinosaurs.

Klutho Studios opened in 1917, was sold to Berg Productions in 1920, and was closed in 1922.

Political reelection of Mayor Bowden was the topic of a December 21, 1916 (page 13, section 2) article "Bowden Club Organized at Big Meeting to Help Reelect Present Mayor." Subhead lines declare that "Enthusiastic Crowd Present Last Evening notwithstanding Inclement Weather. Business Men behind Mayor in His Fight. President of Organization Will Name Executive Committee During Week."

> Friends of Mayor J.E.T. Bowden met last evening on the tenth floor of the Seminole Hotel and formed an organization which will work for his reelection in the coming city primaries. Notwithstanding the inclement weather the hall was well filled and the meeting was the most enthusiastic gathering which has been held during the present campaign by any candidate. Unusual enthusiasm was shown for a political meeting so early in the campaign.
>
> After several speeches had been made, Dave Prince moved that the chairman be empowered to name an executive committee of fifteen. This committee will in turn, cooperating with Mayor Bowden, select a campaign manager. The committee will be selected and given to the press of the city for publication during the present week. Another meeting of the organization perfected last evening will be called by this executive committee as soon as details can be arranged. The chairman will call a meeting of the executive committee as soon as he makes his selections. Work will be started at once and a meeting of the Bowden

club will be called without delay in order that the members may be kept posted as to what is being done and what is needed...

The mayor declared that he had made mistakes as anyone would, but that he was confident that the people believed that he had carried out his preelection pledges and that the city was in a better condition today than it had been for a number of years. His remarks were greeted with applause. Mr. Bowden said he had been informed by friends that Mr. Martin was campaigning among the voters using the argument that he represented the same people who had elected Mr. Bowden two years ago. The mayor asked why a change should be made when the people knew what he would do but had nothing to refer to see what Mr. Martin would do if elected.

Mr. Bowden declared that he favored a well regulated liberal government. He also said that he would not put anything in the way of a man who was trying to make an honest living or enjoy innocent pleasures. He also promised to keep down strife and to cooperate with all departments of the city governments in every way possible.

Richard Garrick was called upon for a speech. He declared that he had talked with all of the producers here and that they were all for Mr. Bowden's reelection. Mr. Garrick declared that the motion picture business was the fourth largest business in the world today and that $10,000,000 was represented in this city at this time by the companies here. He further stated that the New York offices knew that any producer could get anything he wanted in Jacksonville through Mayor Bowden and for that reason they were coming here in larger numbers every year to make pictures. When the speaker declared that Mr. Bowden was responsible for the bringing of the motion picture industry to this city and that he would be glad to contribute to his campaign he was greeted with loud applause.

There were a large number of speakers during the evening among whom were Walter Early, Max Myerson, J.W. Ingram, Dave Prince, W.F. Shine, Richard Garrick and Dr. M.B. Herlong. The mayor expressed the opinion that a whirlwind campaign beginning about ten days before the date of the primary would be the best, but most of the speakers favored getting to work at once. The executive committee will decide upon this point at once. The organization was perfected by the unanimous selection of Ernest Metcalf as president and John Donahue as secretary of the Bowden Campaign Club.

Exactly one month later (*Florida Times-Union*, January 21, 1917, page 8) Mayor J.E.T. Bowden authored the following open letter to the people of Jacksonville. . . .

Two years ago you honored me with election as your mayor, and I feel that I have served you faithfully and to the best of my ability, never turning away from any sensible or friendly suggestion in line with a better administration. Candidly, I ask if you don't think so, too?

Thus, I am stand for reelection 'on my record.' I have no political axes to grind, no plots toward self-evaluation in future above and beyond my local neighborhood calling for possible negotiations in political trades that might prejudice any administration where such ambitions also exist. Everybody knows that my past, present and future on earth is bound up in a single interest—my own dear city of Jacksonville, and your city of Jacksonville, to be the most successful and satisfactory Mayor of this city is my highest and only ambition.

The active alliance against me of powerful and well known political rings, factions and interests proves conclusively that I am not the candidate of any ring, faction or set of men, and that they have not and cannot control me, my administration or its policies.

I have ever stood, and shall ever stand, in readiness to cooperate to the fullest extent with the Governor of Florida, the Sheriff of Duval County and the Federal Authorities in the regulation or suppression of any vicious conditions in Jacksonville, by as vigorous an enforcement of the laws as experience teaches them and myself will result in a ready and continuous betterment of public real cooperation. I am your public servant—not your boss. Get me right in this. My attitude is truly democratic, and I think the people at large will soon understand me better and know, if they do not know, that I am as much alive to the value of the reputation of this or any other city or State or locality for moral and law-abiding citizenship as is the most fastidious and exacting critic of human character.

The regulation of liquor traffic, of course, offers an endless problem to any honest executive, whose personal views, however, have nothing to do with his duty to wisely enforce a law. The official record will bear me out in the assertion that, whereas certain liquor dealers have lawful license to sell liquors at certain times and places, and may not sell on Sundays, I have faithfully enforced the Sunday closing law against all liquor dealers wherever brought to my attention.

In the matter of dealing with prostitution, the best solution my humble judgment has ever suggested to me or others is segregation. Has any other candidate a better suggestion to offer at this time?

I have striven for peace and harmony between all departments, officials and employees of the city government of Jacksonville, as I promised upon taking my seat as Mayor; and if my efforts toward peace and harmony have not been entirely successful, I certainly have not tolerated discord, except in the deference to duty, the performance of which produced discord in the form of opposition to such line of duty. If re-elected, I will continue to fight in line of my official duty, placing all responsibility for discord upon those opposing me in my performance of duties.

My promises made to the people of Jacksonville before my election two years since are a matter of history. My compliance and efforts toward a complete redemption of those promises are matters of city record. In partial fulfillment of a promise to promote extended development of local business enterprise, I did interest, among other industries, a rich, thrifty, cultured and delightful community of incoming producers of moving picture film companies and players, to say nothing of care and encouragement given to local moving picture shows. I feel a just satisfaction in this, and a recent suggestion from the stump that our new citizenship of the film world might take an undue interest in city politics appears to me rather ungracious and uncalled for, while accepting such a valuable industry as part of our city growth and development. Ignoring considerations of culture and refinement, valuable as they are, can we yet afford to ignore and disparage a cash payroll of from $40,000.00 to $50,000.00 a week from the film industry in order to exclude some mighty good new citizenship from our midst?

Most important of my promises to our people on assuming office as your Mayor was a strong, sound business administration. I have tried to give this, and have done better, perhaps, for the city than might have done for myself in any private enterprise. . . .

Yet another political article was to appear on page 3 of the *Florida Times–Union* February 5, 1917 edition. The article, titled "Mayor Bowden Being Villainously Attacked by Candidate Martin in the Same Manner as Martin Attacked United States Senator Fletcher Three Years Ago" was actually a paid advertisement authored by J.E.T. Bowden, candidate for mayor. . . .

From the inception of the present campaign candidate for mayor, John W. Martin has been vilifying me at every opportunity. He has not made a single speech or uttered a single advertisement without attacking me unfairly and untruthfully.

I had made up my mind that I would not pay any attention to these villainous and untruthful attacks, but when he came out in a letter yesterday directed to the voters of the Tenth ward, wherein to the effect that I had gone into the insurance business for the sole purpose of insuring the city property and for no other reason than to prejudice the insurance agents in the city against me, I made up my mind then that I would show up some of these libelous assertions.

I will say that I entered the insurance business purely and simply from a business standpoint, and associated in this business enterprise are such men as Robert W. Gamble, J.Y. Wilson, George M. Powell, Conrad Mangrels, Frederick Auerbach, C.C. Kirby, C.H. Tuteweiler, G.H. Gould, W.K. Jackson, W.A. Elliott and many more influential representative citizens. Mr. Harrison, being a stockholder, elected as business manager of the company, and I will say that this company has not made any effort to secure one dollar's worth of city insurance. It has not written one cent of such insurance, has made no effort to get any of the city insurance, and will not as long as I am connected with the government as mayor.

This company has not been directly or indirectly benefited by any insurance on city property. The books are open to any reputable committee that cares to examine them, and, as I say, this attack is made for no other purpose than to prejudice other insurance agents to vote against me.

In an advertisement of Mr. Martin's appearing in the Times-Union of recent date, which my campaign committee reproduced at my expense, together with a statement of my own appearing the same date, in order that the people could compare same and judge for themselves. Mr. Martin attempts to influence the people by referring to the renting of my property by a dirty little sling in the following words: "What his (Bowden's)—has been rented for by all means LET US THINK." In his attacks over the city he has referred on several occasions to the fact that some of my property was situated in the segregated district, and that I benefited by revenue from that class of people. I want to say right here that these charges have been made against me from one campaign to another, and I have never paid any attention to such charges, but I wish to emphatically announce that I do not own a single piece of property , not even an inch of ground in what is termed as the segregated district: that I have never owned but one lot in that locality, which I took for debt many years ago, and which I have disposed of a long time since however, a great number of people in Jacksonville are under the impression that I do own such property, and I will give $1,000 to any man who will show where I own, directly or indirectly, one single foot of ground on the street south of Adams and west of Broad , which is generally known as the under-world district.

Mr. Martin has on many occasions attacked me as being a negro lover: inciting the unthinking minds against me: insinuating that I have addressed the negroes on familiar terms, and that I was making them my social equal. These assertions, Mr. Martin knows, and every self respecting man in Jacksonville knows is absolutely false: in other words—"LIES CUT FROM THE WHOLE CLOTH."

He is also making a desperate effort to incite the workingman against me on account of my doing my duty as I saw it. In carrying out my oath of office a mayor on the occasion of the recent so-called street railway strike, which was no strike to those employed, but a strike brought on by agitators in order to fill their pockets as walking delegates, etc. I want to ask the working people of this city—those who have come here recently—to ask the old citizens who have lived here for years what I have done for organized labor and the poor man generally. I wish Mr. Martin would point to one solitary act, either privately or publicly, where he has turned one straw for their benefit. I would further ask him to show one public act of his that would entitle him to the confidence of our people, entitling him to the office of mayor.

Three years ago Mr. Martin attacked in the same villainous manner our present United States senator, Duncan U. Fletcher going over the state making untruthful and outrageous charges against a man of his standing and character.—still he has the audacity to ask our people to elevate him to this high office on such tactics.

The people of Jacksonville have honored me time and time again. They have elected me mayor over and over again, as well as councilman. I would not have been reelected to these positions had I not had the confidence and respect of my people, so I cannot sit idly by any longer and allow my character assailed by an unknown—this man who has never accomplished one thing for the public—or for the benefit of the people, to vilify me in the outrageous manner in which he is now doing. I have made it a rule of my life never to attack my opponent's character or in any other way that would reflect upon him as a citizen: where I have differed with my opponents I have only attacked their public records and ideas on public questions.

I want to say that I am not a candidate this time of my own choosing, and I would not today be in this race were it not for the fact that a committee of twenty representing the entire business interests of the city came to my office and urged me to run. At the time I told this committee that I felt I had done my full duty for my city, but they argued until finally I consented to be a candidate for reelection. Now that I am a candidate, I ask my people to endorse my administration by reelecting me to this office. I have tried my best to do my duty by Jacksonville and every citizen in it, no matter how high or lowly his position. I have been at my desk continually since my induction into office attending to the business interests of Jacksonville, and I can point with pride to the accomplishments of this administration. Mr. Martin is claiming that I had nothing to do with the present magnificent financial condition of the city, so I simply refer the people of Jacksonville to the voluntary letter given me by Treasurer Alexander Ray upon presenting to me, as chairman of the finance commission and as mayor his yearly report for 1916, which is within itself the most flattering statement ever made, and Treasurer Ray, who has been connected with the Treasure's office for nearly twenty years, assures me over his signature that it is the most flattering statement he has ever had the pleasure of presenting. He also told me at the time of presenting the statement that it was not his custom with such letters, but that he felt on account of the constructive work the way I had handled affairs and worked with him and any other officials that he felt the people should know what had been accomplished by a constructive business administration. He has on many occasions told me to refer any citizen to him as to the manner in which I had cooperated with the departments in my efforts to reduce expenditures and save the people's money.

I came to Jacksonville when I was a small boy, and have worked my way from the very bottom round of the ladder without influence or money behind me to the position that I now occupy as a successful business man and a successful servant of the people, and I have not forgotten the days when I was poor and when I had to struggle for a living, economizing in every possible way in order to get a start in life and my efforts as an officer have been for the betterment of the man who could not take care of himself.

Mr. Martin has also undertaken to vilify each coworker with me. He has attacked my campaign manager, my business partner and those who have voluntarily taken the stump for me in such a manner as should blacken him and run from him every self- respecting voter of this city. I have never known of a candidate being successful who tried to force himself into office over the corpse of his opponent and his coworkers have attended my meetings trying to break up the same by rowdy's: on the other hand, those who have espoused my cause have been most respectful when attending his meetings, notwithstanding the villainous insults he has heaped upon me. Such men as Messrs. Joe Sherouse, Ike Harmon, both of whom have known me not less than thirty years, know the work that I have done in the interest of the poor man and for these reasons they have espoused my cause. He comes out in an advertisement wherein he says that "Mr. Sherouse who a few days ago was denouncing Mayor Bowden has certainly changed after seeing his manager." Now, I challenge him or any other man to bring forward one single solitary citizen who can impugn Mr. Sherouse's character. He is a man who is fearless and has always stood for the right, and today is espousing my cause because he believes I am the best man for the office, and my private and public acts have been of such character as to convince him that I am an officer recognizing all of the people, and that the poor man—the man in overalls—as well as the fellow clad in broadcloth can reach me at any time.

Now I am asking the thinking man, the voter who is interested in the upbuilding of this city, to look at conditions today and contrast them with those of two years ago as far as a lively city is concerned: to compare the statement as made over Treasurer Ray's signature of what has been accomplished: THINK and reason with yourself, see if it would not be foolish to make an experiment now while Jacksonville is on the upward road to prosperity, the financial and moral interests of the city are being protected most thoroughly: politics have had no part in my administration: on the other hand, I have worked for the benefit of Jacksonville, and every citizen, therefore, ask them to THINK and THINK and THINK before placing in office a man without a record except as a salesman and recently admitted to the bar, that hardly anyone knew of, until he suddenly jumped into notoriety three years ago in vilifying the Hon. Duncan U. Fletcher the same as he is doing to me now.

I don't believe the people of Jacksonville are ungrateful: I don't believe that they wish to take a step backward and I don't believe that they are an unthinking people. The business interests today are to a man with me, but most of those opposing me are simply those who have been preyed upon by misrepresentation and harangues that have nothing to do with municipal government and should have no part in government.

Now voters, I again ask you to think and think well before placing your cross in front of the candidate for mayor tomorrow. Think if you would turn out a faithful servant who carries out your wishes—or in other words his promises—to work for you and to work for the city you are most interested in—YOUR CITY, MY CITY, and put in harness a man who has never turned his hand to better governmental or political conditions but on the other hand has been stirring up strife, arraying the unthinking class against the very best citizens that Jacksonville can boast of.

I am asking you to THINK before casting your vote. I am going to submit my candidacy to you. This is the last line I expect to write on the subject. I am in your hands, and it is all up to you to continue a progressive business administration or take the chance of having this city in the condition it was before I took office.

Very respectfully,
J.E.T. Bowden
Candidate for Mayor.

Candidate Bowden faced not only his opposition, John W. Martin, but also circumstances were against him. (Martin would go on after being elected to become governor of Florida in the 1920's.) Three events conspired against his candidacy and all the good that he had accomplished. These three events are aptly described by the Jacksonville Historical Society in a book, published in 1947, as previously referred to at the start of this chapter.

In 1916 there were some 30 or so movie companies operating in Jacksonville. It is interesting to note that none of these problems involved the comedy companies spotlighted by this book, yet they were to affect the whole future of J.E.T. Bowden's encouragement of the film industry in Jacksonville as a whole. . . .

> The magic of the silver screen lured many Jacksonville residents to the studios and an almost all-Jacksonville cast was chosen for the filming of The Clarion by the Equitable Company in 1916 . . . Carlyle Blackwell was the star of The Clarion and Clifford Robertson was the company manager. In all, 1,380 Jacksonville men and boys took part in the 'mob' scene, during which a two-story building and saloon at Davis and Monroe Streets were almost completely destroyed. Also used were 40 policemen, who rushed in and swung away with rubber clubs.
>
> Because the 'mob' became unruly and almost uncontrollable, it gave a tainted name to motion picture producing and furnished fuel for those who had opposed the film industry being here all along. From then on opposition to the film producers gained in strength.
>
> In filming The Dead Alive, a spectacular dash of a big automobile down Main Street with a plunge into the river from the ferry dock was featured. This scene, with over 100 Jacksonville people taking part, was taken last, owing to the possibility of some unforeseen effect upon the players as a result of the dip into the water. However, the 'reckless' dash and other such scenes of cars weaving in and out of downtown traffic were pointed to by the film opponents as unsafe to the public. There were other 'incidents,' too, such as turning in an alarm to bring out fire engines when needed for a scene; shooting of 'bank robberies' on Sundays when there were fewer people in the streets, and advertising a parachute jump from the top of the Graham Building for several days in order to draw a crowd necessary to complete a picture.
>
> Opposition to Bowden came in the form of a lawyer named John Martin, who was supported by a group of citizens who did not favor the changes that had taken place since the movie industry came to Jacksonville. The Jacksonville Historical Society, in their 1947 publication, had this to say about the election.
> . . .
> . . . the motion picture industry became an issue in the city election, and candidates backed by opponents of the cinema people won. About that time, D.W. Griffith's immortal Birth of a Nation, which had been filmed in California, met with wide success and producers began eyeing wonders of the West Coast with envy.

Still another factor that seemed to work against Jacksonville was the organization of the Famous Player Lasky Corporation, which signed up most of all the top names of the day, and the old Patents Company group fell apart. Edison, Kalem, Lubin and Biograph, glorious in their day, had shut down and quit. Gaumont, French Company, closed down when the United States entered World War I. Discouraged by the lack of cooperation received here and attracted by inducements from California film successes, one by one the studios here closed up, and before long all had left and gone to California to make a new film capital in Hollywood.

Almost overnight, it seems, Jacksonville became a 'ghost town,' so far as motion picture productions were concerned. . . .

Further details are provided in Richard Allen Nelson's fall 1980 article, "Movie Mecca of the South: Jacksonville, Florida as an Early Rival to Hollywood," as published in the *Journal of Popular Film and Television*. In this article Mr. Nelson has this to say about Jacksonville's election of 1917 and its consequences. . . .

This simmering controversy over the movie colony became a hot political issue in Mayor Bowden's 1917 re-election campaign. Pitted against the mayor was a coalition of 'reform' interest (churches, prohibitionists, anti-vice crusaders and others) who coalesced around lawyer John Martin as their candidate. When Bowden received the almost unanimous support of the local studios (who had approximately $10,000,000 invested in the city), Martin reacted bitterly by saying that while personally he wasn't against moviemaking coming to Jacksonville "he did not want them to get into local politics." This struck a responsive chord with many voters and Martin won a startling upset against the heavily favored Bowden. The reaction was immediate, and "a cinematic chill pervaded the once-warm climate." The sudden reversal in mood was evidenced among the producers as well as the voting public. Richard Garrick stunned the city by announcing his immediate departure from Jacksonville and the closing of his studios. . . .

While Bowden's defeat split the city by removing the area's major 'movie booster' from power, this alone would not have destroyed the local industry. Other factors impinged to cause the closure of most of the local studios. The final breakup of the member studios which had been glorious in their day— Kalem, Selig, and Lubin among them—had continued to rely on short films as their bread-and-butter output of their firms. But before the end of 1918, they all were forced to shut down entirely and sell off their assets. The failure of their managements to foresee public demand for features, the precipitous changeover of the two-reel comedy from a staple to lesser importance on playbills, the imposition of costly new taxes, the closing of foreign markets to some of the more marginal producers, and shortages of raw stock all combined to form the death blow. At the same time, price gouging by Jacksonville merchants, the refusal of local banks to play much of a role in financing Florida-made pictures, a deadly influenza epidemic, unseasonable freezing weather, and general apathy helped to drive most of the remaining active producers away.

In effect, both Jacksonville and New York were abandoned as production centers by the major producers at the end of World War I. Production was concentrated on the West Coast where studios were expanded, economic controls could be more efficiently maintained, and conditions proved ideal. The trend towards diffusion that had dominated the industry since its origins was now reversed, and this marks the clear rise of Hollywood in the public mind to its preeminence as the world's leading motion picture metropolis.

Mayor Bowden, the movie industry advocate, was out due to the change in the climate of opinion by the people of Jacksonville. The more conservative John Martin was in and the city started to be less welcoming to the movie industry.

When the conservative faction was victorious, presumably Jacksonville went back to the way it had been before the movie companies arrived.

John Martin was Mayor of Jacksonville for two terms before running successfully for governor in the 1920's. It is not known what happened to Mayor Bowden. Seemingly overnight the movie companies left Jacksonville, and gravitated back to Hollywood. Yet on July 2, 1920 a curious article appeared on the Volume 59.6 issue of *Variety*, it was entitled Picture People's Grievances Against Los Angeles Aired . . . .

> Los Angeles, June 30, representatives of the picture industry last week presented their grievance against elements and influences in Los Angeles. The hearers who also proved to be friends and advisors were men as representative of business interests as they of picture producing industry. It was a remarkable season of unbosoming. The producers did not use velvet words. They told their story in a straight-out way and let it go at that.
>
> The meeting was called by the Chamber of Commerce in its headquarters. Besides the producers, there were bankers, merchants and manufacturers and a number of newspapermen around the table.
>
> The charges were of two kinds; that there is an undercurrent of prejudice in Los Angeles against people engaged in the picture business which crops out in 'condescension' the refusal of landlords to rent to them, and the general grouping, in the rent scheme, with babies, animals and other undesirables.
>
> The other count is financial. This includes the matter of exorbitant rents to film people, unfair assessments by the county assessor and higher prices charged by Los Angeles merchants than the public pays. Here are the charges, in more detail, which the meeting brought forth:
> 1. The county assessor appraises moving picture cameras, light machinery and electrical devices 5 per cent higher than is assessed against other businesses.

2. Many landlords are prejudiced against all persons connected with the picture industry and class them with dogs, monkeys and babies. If they do rent, they charge exorbitantly.
3. Los Angeles stores from which 'props' are rented value their wares at 10 per cent above prices to the public.
4. The matter of publicity. If a film actor or actress does something bizarre or is the victim of unfortunate circumstances, the facts are good for a first page sensation, whereas if the same things befall an ordinary citizen, the story gets an obscure item next to the classified 'ads.'
5. Furthermore, many people affect an attitude of condescension toward moving picture makers.

On the part of the merchants and other business men present, it was held that the picture producers have not cooperated with them, that the industry has been in the state of disorganization, that the prejudices of some landlords and the outrageous rentals stand for the attitude of individuals and not the city.

Maynard McFie, president of the Chamber, opened the proceedings with a word of appreciation that Los Angeles is the picture capital of the world. He said he called the meeting because charges had been made against merchants, landlords and others by picture people, and the Chamber wanted to find out the facts, discover a remedy and apply it.

L.J. Loeb, attorney for a number of producers, brought out the complaint on assessments. "I do not know on what theory the county assessor makes the distinction," he said, "but it is a fact, for purpose of taxation he values picture property five per cent higher."

By October 13, 1920, word that some movie companies were dissatisfied with Los Angeles got back to Jacksonville, prompting the following article on page 4 of *The Florida Metropolis*. . . .

There is no reason why Jacksonville should not become one of the leading motion picture producing centers in the country.

The city is ideally located for this industry, and to list all of the advantages would require a detailed report from an expert; but producers who have visited Jacksonville state this is a natural location for motion picture work. Ideal climate would make it possible for the open air studio to operate twelve months in the year; the city is accessible by rail and water to all parts of the country—and is the stepping stone to Florida, a state with unequalled scenic possibilities for immediate use in motion pictures. No preparations are necessary. Nature has attended to that.

And now that the Chamber of Commerce is beginning to take real steps towards attracting companies to this section, the business and civic interests of the city should line up squarely behind the chamber and offer assistance at every end. If success is to crown the effort, cooperation must be manifested and it will be a reflection of the community spirit for the people to permit the movement to die without first giving it unlimited support—with enthusiasm and with financial backing.

Too long have we accepted our many natural resources and not given enough attention to the potentialities waiting to become realities, if we will only say the word; and no doubt being progressive and interested in the future advancement of this city, the influential people of Jacksonville will lend a helping hand to the Chamber of Commerce in this work. It is a business proposition—one from that standpoint which will bring millions of dollars here yearly, one which calls for capital from outside investors as well as here at home, but, in our opinion, that is a secondary although important consideration.

Jacksonville has something to offer. The transaction is legitimate. To have it accepted means wonderful things for the city.

Let's make Jacksonville a motion picture center!

Finally, on November 12, 1920, an unidentified "prominent film man" was interviewed by the *Florida Times-Union* (section 2, first page) for an article titled "Motion Picture Industry Has A Warm Welcome For Jacksonville."

"The motion picture industry welcomes Jacksonville as the third motion picture producing center," declares prominent film man in an interview with Motion Picture News, one of the important trade publications.

Preferring not to have his name mentioned at this time, one of the industry's most prominent men gives some light on the subject and speaks freely as to conditions existing in California. Why Florida has wonderful possibilities of interesting the trade and reasons why Florida will succeed in her endeavors, are a few of the points discussed.

One who might almost be called a commuter between the west coast of California and New York was met in his spacious suite at the Hotel Astor, New York, almost immediately after he had arrived from Los Angeles. Although the gentleman was very busy with his secretary, it was only necessary to put one question to him to obtain his full interest. When asked to tell something about California, a rapid line of conversation followed immediately.

"Productions cost more than ever," said our man from the coast. We can't keep expenses down under any formula. If the expense of making pictures continues to rise, we will have to find some other producing center other than California . . . Los Angeles practically lives off the motion picture industry and yet they overlook this fact in dragging out of us every dollar they possibly can.

I can't figure the attitude the merchants in Los Angeles are taking toward producers. Without the picture industry where would Los Angeles stand in comparison to other cities? Still they do everything possible to discourage the motion picture producer in staying in this city. My production costs are mounting continually and we cannot hold them down. We have tried every possible way to cut our expenses but the whole thing resolves itself to the one fact that in Los Angeles they use the picture people for a good thing. Every merchant takes advantage of us by boosting his price on any article the moment he learns the purchase is for the producer. I have known of instances where department stores have two prices marked on their tags. These prices are marked in code: naturally impossible for anyone to know the real price. The higher price is used for the picture people and the lower for those not connected with the industry.

In Los Angeles the picture people, that is, the stars, the directors, producers etc., are known to all the merchants: when they enter a store to buy, the merchant immediately quotes them a higher price. To illustrate this fact one of our stars purchased a piece of jewelry in one of the downtown shops. She is prominently known among the merchants. Her friend later in the week bought another just like the one the star purchased at the same place and paid 50 per cent less.

"You will agree," he continued, "this is the wrong attitude in regard to the picture people since they are always ready and good spenders. This increase in price to picture people places the burden entirely on the producer, for in the end we the producers are the ones who have to foot the bill for the high cost of living. This attitude also applies when we buy materials to be used in the studios. . . .

When the subject of Jacksonville as a third producing center was brought to his attention he became very interested, and wanted to know all about Florida's activities in relation to the motion picture industry. I believe Jacksonville has wonderful possibilities interesting the motion picture industry in coming to Florida to establish there a new center for producing motion pictures. The fact that the Famous Players Corporation has just completed their studio in Long Island gives reason to believe that the South will come into its own as a producing center. I say this for this reason: With such big studios as the Famous Players Corporation control in New York, in order to grow they will have to travel for their locations. This means they will have to go to the far west or to the south.

Now then, if the South will show the industry reasonable cause to locate there in the winter they can easily accomplish another producing center. There are many producing companies on the coast who would gladly locate in Jacksonville if the proposition is put to them in a forcible way.

In so far as scenery is concerned, I believe Florida offers everything needed for making pictures. It is true that Jacksonville is not backed up by mountains. In a majority of pictures that are made, mountains are not necessary and when necessary to take such mountain scenes, a short ride to the Carolinas will furnish all the mountain locations necessary. Besides this, the scenery will be new to the theater-going public, and it is the new things that count in picture making.

If you intend to print this article I would ask you not to mention my name in connection with it, but you can feel sure that the motion picture industry welcomes Jacksonville as the third producing center."

Circumstances conspired against Jacksonville yet again, preventing the city from becoming a third film production center. In October of 1920, the Jacksonville Chamber of Commerce created a motion picture committee to be in charge of developing this. However the city council refused to advance the Jacksonville Chamber the $5,745 it needed for advertising. Only after a prolonged debate was the funding finally approved.

On January 1, 1921 plans for a Fine Arts Center, to be built at nearby Camp Johnston by Fine Arts Pictures Incorporated, were released. However the financial backing for this project, from New York City, never materialized.

The plans got a second chance when Lewis J. Selznick stepped in, with a plan to design a studio that would be built by architect John Klutho. When these plans failed, so too did Jacksonville's future as a third center of film production.

Richard Allen Nelson's fall 1980 article, "Movie Mecca of the South: Jacksonville, Florida as an Early Rival to Hollywood," (as published in the *Journal of Popular Film and Television*) commented on developments of the 1920's. . . .

> With opportunities for Jacksonville to develop as a post-war production location site severely limited and the city a virtual ghost town, local proponents made a last ditched effort in the early 1920s to reacquire a large portion of the industry. Only after strained debate, however, were city funds appropriated or a trade advertising campaign stressing Jacksonville as veritable celluloid heaven . . . Jacksonville never again offered a serious challenge to California. Although at one time it was the movie Mecca of the South, it soon became just another forgotten rival to Hollywood.

So ends the story of Jacksonville's brief bid to become the Hollywood of the South. Hollywood, California would become the center of motion picture production and later television productions.

Today there is very little left in Jacksonville to tell the interesting tale of Jacksonville's rich film history. We have chosen here to show it through the genre of silent film comedy, which is a major interest of mine. Hopefully I have succeeded in this endeavor.

It is interesting to note that an organization called Old Arlington. Inc, a community revitalization program, and the Norman Studios historic preservation project have undertaken to restore the site. Norman Studios is where the Eagle Film Company was located.

An article called "Before Hollywood, There Was Jacksonville: Preserving Florida's Filmmaking Heritage," in the winter 2004 issue, page 21, was the following. . . .

> After Arlington resident Ann Burt discovered the hidden past of the old wooden building in her neighborhood, she resolved to share their history. As the focus of Old Arlington, Inc.'s (OAI) community revitalization effort, she and other members of the organization succeeded in saving the site.
>
> "We want people to know Florida's role in the establishment of the movie industry," says Burt. "More than that, we want to tell the story of the Africa American movie experience as Richard Norman presented it. Besides providing

entertainment for African American audiences, his films such as The Flying Ace and The Bull Dagger served as an antidote to the racism of the times."

Last April the city purchased four of the original Norman studios buildings. The structures that once housed sets, props, a 1905-vintage generator, and other moviemaking facilities have seen other uses since Norman's death. The old production building still contains the original darkroom, screening and projection rooms, and walk-in safe for storing films. Water scenes were filmed in a swimming pool now buried on the site. OAI has efforts underway to obtain funding and support to begin needed restoration and preservation activities.

Florida's role in the history of film is being commemorated by several dedicated individuals and institutions, a new scholarship program honors Norman's legacy and celebrates filmmaking in the state today.

Yet another local repository of artifacts from Norman Studios (and by extension Eagle Films) is at Jacksonville's Museum of Science and History, 1025 Museum Circle, Jacksonville. It, and the Arlington restoration of Norman studios, are avenues yet unexplored by this writer.

This book manuscript would be lacking if it did not include mention of the primary first hand knowledge source of information used in this book. The Florida Room of the main public library is an entrance point to the early 1900's film history of Jacksonville. By using the early issues of the *Florida Times-Union* and *Metropolis* newspapers, and having specific articles to access, it was possible to recreate over time important elements of the film history. Even though this book covers only a limited number of the reported 30 film companies (thought to be filming in Jacksonville in Jacksonville in 1916) it is thought to be sufficient to describe the circumstances. It remains for some other writer to document other studios that operated here.

The author gratefully acknowledges the assistance of the Florida Room staff, and my research assistant Carol K. Farrell, in obtaining the information necessary to complete this manuscript.

If one would venture a guess, it would be that most people have never thought about Jacksonville's part in the history of moviemaking, much less that it once was a rival of Hollywood, California. Hopefully this book has illustrated that Jacksonville was once, long ago, for one brief period of time, almost Hollywood.

Bibliography

BOOKS

Barlow, Margaret. *Before Hollywood, There was Jacksonville: Preserving Florida's Filmmaking Heritage.* Artifacts from Museum of Florida History, Mosh, and Arlington, Inc. date unknown.

Bell, Geoffrey. *The Golden Gate and the Silver Screen: San Francisco in the History of the Cinema.* Cranbury, NJ: Associated University Presses, 1984.

Gold, Pleasant Daniel. *History of Duval County Florida.* St. Augustine, Florida, 1928.

James, William R. *Arlington: A New History, Old Arlington Inc.* Jacksonville, Florida: City of Jacksonville, 1996.

Lahue, Kalton C. and Gill, Sam. *Clown Princes and Court Jesters: Some Great Comics of the Silent Screen.* A.S. Barnes and Co., Inc., Cranbury, New Jersey.

Leslie-Judge Company. *Film Flashes: The Wit and Humor of a Nation in Pictures.* Leslie-Judge Company, 1916.

McCabe, John. *Babe: The Life of Oliver Hardy.* Citadel Press, 1989.

Miller, Blair. *American Silent Film Comedies: An Illustrated Encyclopedia of Persons, Studios and Terminology.* Jefferson, North Carolina and London: McFarland and Company, Inc., Publishers. 1995.

Motion Picture News. *Motion Picture Studio Directory and Trade Annual.* Motion Picture News, Inc., 729 Seventh Avenue, New York City. Also Chicago and Los Angeles, 1920.

Nelson, Richard Alan. *Florida and the American Motion Picture Industry*, 1898-1930 (Volumes One and Two), Ann Arbor, Michigan: UMI Dissertation Services, copyright 1980. Reprinted in 1997 by UMI.

Skretvedt, Randy. *Laurel and Hardy: The Magic Behind the Movies.* Beverly Hills, California: Moonstone Press, 1987.

Stone, Rob. *Laurel or Hardy: The Solo Films of Stan Laurel and Oliver "Babe" Hardy.* Temecula, California: Split Reel Books, 1996.

Ward, James Robertson and Snodgrass, Dena Elizabeth. *Old Hickory's Town: an Illustrated History of Jacksonville*. Old Hickory's Town, Incorporated, Jacksonville, Florida, 1985.

Wood, Wayne W., Tool, Stephen Joseph Jr. and McEachin, Joel Wright. *Jacksonville's Architectural Heritage: Landmarks for the Future.* University Press of Florida, 1996.

PERIODICALS

Lights! Camera! Florida! Ninety Years of Moviemaking and Television Production in the Sunshine State. *The Florida Endowment for the Humanities*, February 1987, Tampa, Florida.

Nelson, Richard Allen. "Movie Mecca of the South: Jacksonville, Florida as an Early Rival to Hollywood." *Journal of Popular Film and Television*, Vol. VIII, #3, Fall 1980, pages 38-51.

Nelson, Richard Allen. "Before Laurel: Oliver Hardy and the Vim Company, A Studio Biography," Current Research in Film (Volume 2), ed. by Bruce A. Austin. Norwood, NJ. *Abelex Publishing Corporation*, 1986, pages 136-155.

Nelson, Richard Alan. "Movie Mecca of the South: Jacksonville, Florida as an Early Rival to Hollywood" pps.38-51.

Webb, Stephen R. "Klever Komedies in the Great War: One Studio's Contribution to the War Effort." *Film History*, Volume 3, pp. 105-113, 1989.

CD-ROM

Thanhouser Films: An Encyclopedia and History, by Q. David Bowers, The Complete History of the Silent Film Studio from 1909 to 1918. This is a CD-Rom for IBM compatible PCs with Windows 95. Copyright 1997 by Thanhouser Company Film Preservation, Inc.

JOURNALS

"Debut of Sparkle Comedies." *Motography: Exploiting Motion Pictures,* Vol.18, 1, (1917): 123.

"In Old Florida—Kalem." *Motography: Exploiting Motion Pictures,* Vol. 5, 5, (1911): 97.

"Jacksonville Entertains Kessel." *Motography: Exploiting Motion Pictures,* Vol. 17, 3, (1917): 149.

"Jacksonville Helps Producers." *Motography: Exploiting Motion Pictures,* Vol.15, 14, (1916): 735.

"Laugh Even in the Making of a Comedy." *Motography: Exploiting Motion Pictures,* Vol. 19, 7, (1918): 310.

"Moore Establishes New Studio." *Motography: Exploiting Motion Pictures,* Vol. 18, 1, (1917): 40.

"Moore to Increase His Klever Komedies." *Motography: Exploiting Motion Pictures,* Vol. 32, 13, (1917): 2125.

"Paramount's Klever Komedies." *Motography: Exploiting Motion Pictures,* Vol. 16, 23, (1916): 1240.

"Pokes and Jabbs Popular." *Motography: Exploiting Motion Pictures,* Vol.17, 17 (1917): 896.

"Story of a Fat Boy." *Motography: Exploiting Motion Pictures,* (1916):1211.

"The Call of Jacksonville." *Motography: Exploiting Motion Pictures,* Vol. 15, 11, (1916): 587.

NEWSPAPERS

"Babe Hardy, the Fat Boy with Vim," *Florida Metropolis,* February 20, 1916, p. 5C.

"Bowden Club Organized at Big Meeting to Help Reelect Present Mayor," *Florida Times-Union,* sec. 2December 21, 1916, p.13.

"Busy Jax" to be the subject of Picture Play," *Florida Times-Union,* March 21, 1912, p.13.

"Committee to Advertise Jax as Movie Field," *Florida Metropolis,* October 7, 1920, p. 15.

"Delegation May Be Sent to New York to Get California Motion Picture Industries," *Florida Times-Union,* sec. 2, January 12, 1916, p. 13.

"Eagle Company is working on Big Features," *Florida Metropolis,* January 11, 1916, p. 14.

"Elsie MacLeod is Writing a Scenario for a Big Concern," *Florida Times-Union,* May 3, 1916, p. 3.

"Ferdinand Perez as Tweedledum in an Eagle Production in which he plays Fourteen Characters," *Florida Metropolis,* April 30, 1916, p.12C.

"Film Industry and City Have Close History," *Florida Times-Union,*December 27, 1964, p.14E.

"Finest Movie Studio in South to Open in December" *Florida Times-Union,* November 5, 1915, p.15.

"Garrick Changes Hours of Sunday Picture Making," *Florida Times-Union,* November 24, 1915, p. 12.

"Garrick Says Producers of Motion Pictures Must Have Co-operation to Stay Here," *Florida Times-Union,* November 14, 1915, p. 10.

"Garrick Studio is start for Jax to Eclipse the Los Angeles Picture Colony," *Florida Times-Union,* sec. 2, July 5, 1916, p. 11.

"Genuine Welcome is Extended to Movie Industry," *Florida Times-Union,* February 11, 1916, p. 10.

"Great Movie Ball Planned for Benefit of Two Charities," *Florida Times-Union*, sec. 2, March 17, 1916, p. 13.

"Historic film studio gets termite treatment," by John Carter. *Florida Times-Union*, March 24, 2004, p. 2W.

"Hotel Roseland," *Florida Times-Union*, March 5, 1905, p. 22.

"In Winter Home Kalem People a Happy Bunch," *Florida Times-Union*, December 26, 1911, p.11.

"Jacksonville, Florida, The New York of the South," *Florida Times-Union*, sec. 3, December 6, 1908, pps.4-5.

"Jax and Motion Pictures," *Florida Metropolis*, October 13, 1920, p.4.

"Jax Newsweekly is devoted to Movie People," *Florida Metropolis*, April 19, 1916.

"Jax Pioneers who are still active," *Florida Metropolis*, November 5, 1920, p.3.

"Jax to Offer Many Inducements to Movie Producers," *Florida Metropolis*, May 14, 1916, p. 5D.

"Jax will Become the Hub of Motion Picture Industry...--If ?" *Florida Times-Union*, sec. 3, February 6, 1916, p. 9.

"Jax's Growth," *Florida Times-Union*, January 12, 1917, p.12.

"Jax's Industries," *Florida Times-Union*, December 16, 1915, p.10.

"Kalem Company Arrives for Winter Season," *Florida Times-Union*, October 6, 1912, p. 13.

"Kalem Family Arrives," *Florida Times-Union*, October 20. 1913, p. 8.

"Kalem Stars Arrive to Work at Local Studio," *Florida Times-Union*, September 6, 1916, p.12.

"Louis Burstein is to show films of 5 Committeemen," *Florida Times-Union*, sec. 1, January 23, 1916, p. 4.

"Lubin Company Left for Philadelphia," *Florida Times-Union*, April 30, 1913, p. 15.

"Lubin Company to Return to Jax," *Florida Times-Union*, October 8, 1912, p.11.

"Lubin Studio to be used by Ocean Film Co," *Florida Metropolis*, October 19, 1913, p. 10.

"Many Want to Induce Movie People Back to City Again," *Florida Times-Union*, sec. 1, July 2, 1916, p. 4.

"Mayor Bowden and Officers of civic Bodies Invite Moving Picture Makers to Jax," *Florida Metropolis*, January 23, 1916, p. 6C.

"Mayor Bowden Being Villainously Attacked by Candidate Martin ..." *Florida Times-Union*, February 5, 1917, p. 3.

"Motion Picture Industry has Warm Welcome for Jax," *Florida Times-Union*, November 12, 1920, p. 13.

"Motion Picture Men Hail Jax as Klondike of this Growing Industry," *Florida Times-Union*, sec. 2, March 15, 1916, p. 17.

"Motion Picture of Jax will be an Excellent Ad," *Florida Metropolis*, February 15, 1916, section 2, p. 1.

"Movie Men Here Have Organized a Cinema Club," *Florida Times-Union*, sec. 1, October 1, 1916, p. 10.

"Movie of Jax to be shown the N.Y. Producers," *Florida Metropolis*, January 13, 1916, p. 1.

"Movie of this City is being Made by Experts," *Florida Metropolis,* January 15, 1916, no page given.

"Nat C. Goodwin and his Mirror Film Players use Jax as stage for Funny Comedy..." *Florida Times-Union,* sec. 1, February 27, 1916, p. 9.

"Nat Goodwin Declares that Motion Pictures..." *Florida Times-Union,* sec. 2, February 22, 1916, p.15.

"New York Movie Co. Buys Klutho..." *Florida Times-Union,* July 28, 1920, p. 11.

"Old Vim Concern Bawled up in Finances," *Florida Times-Union,* November 7, 1916, p. 14.

"Rapid and Remarkable Growth of City as Amusement Center," *Florida Times-Union,* sec. 2, November 22, 1908, p. 1.

"Scenes at the Vim Studio," *Florida Times-Union,* sec. 3, January 16, 1916, p. 5.

"Scenes of Action in the Thanhouser Plant/ Popular Members of the Local Thanhouser Co." *Florida Times-Union,* sec. 3, January 16, 1916, pps. 8-9.

"Screen Club to Be Perfected at Meeting November 16," *Florida Times-Union,* sec. 2,November 3, 1916, p. 9.

"Screen Club was organized Last evening," *Florida Times-Union,* sec. 2, November 18, 1916, p. 14.

"Thanhouser Co. in Jacksonville Ready for Work," *Florida Times-Union,* sec. 4, December 26, 1915, p. 14.

"Thanhouser Co. in Jax Ready for Work," *Florida Times-Union,* sec. 4, December 26, 1915, p. 14.

"Thanhouser Film Co. Opens Studio January 1," *Florida Times-Union,* sec. 2, December 3, 1916, p. 21.

"Thanhouser Topics," *Florida Metropolis,* March 5, 1916, p. 8C.

"Thanhouser's are Here to Work at Studio on 8th Street," *Florida Times-Union,* December 21, 1915, p. 11.

"Thanhouser's are Ready for a Great Season Here in City," *Florida Times-Union,* sec. 1, December 26, 1915, p. 6.

"Thanhouser to Close Studio During the Week," *Florida Times-Union,* sec. 2, May 21, 1916, p. 13.

"Thanhouser to Resume Operation October 15," *Florida Times-Union,* September 16, 1916, p. 3.

"The Story of Jacksonville," *Florida Times-Union,* sec. 1, July 17, 1921, p. 5.

"The United States Film Corporation," *Florida Times-Union,* sec. 2, October 8, 1916, p. 22.

"To the People of Jax." *Florida Times-Union,* January 21, 1917, p. 8.

"To the People of Jax and Florida," *Florida Times-Union,* sec. 1, January 16, 1921, p. 7.

"Tweedledum Comedies Being Made in Jax by the Vim Co," *Florida Times-Union,* January 30, 1916, p. 10.

"Vim Comedy Players Lease Lubin Studios," *Florida Times-Union,* November 4, 1915, p. 3.

Index

Actor's Home on Staten Island, 25
Albertson, Arthur, 15, 34, 36, 38
Amber Star comedies, 54, 55, 56, 57–59, 108, 112, 113

Bletcher, Billy, 46, 52, 55–56
Black Diamond studios, 96, 111
Bowden, J.E.T., 14–27, 70, 113–22
Burns, Bobby, 46–47, *50–51,* 51, 55, 59
Burns, Robert, 46, 47, 55
Burstein, Louis, 15, 19, 20, 22, 27, 45–47, 54, 58, 60–63, 66

Candler Building/Asa Candler, 58
Casino Star, 42
Chamberlain, Riley, 21, 83
Clarkson Street, 32
Close, Ivy, 28, 31
Cohan, Margerie, 38

Dintenfass, Mark, 15, 20, 45, 54, 58, 111
Dixieland Park, 57, 104, *105, 106,* 108–9
Dramatic Mirror (The New York), 76

Eagle Film Company, 16–20, 67–73, 126, 127
Eastern Film Company, 57–59, 108

Eastman Kodak Building, New York City, 28
Edison, Thomas, 108 Edison Company, 42, 52, 56, 58, 90, 108, 111, 112, 121; Patent Trust, 35, 40
Ellis, Robert, 34
Encore Pictures Corporation, 104

Falstaff comedies, 74–75, 79, *81,* 83, 85, 87, 89, 90, 91–94
Finn and Haddie comedies, 58
Florence, Minerva, 36
Florida Ostrich and Alligator Farm, 104, *106–7,* 108
Florida Metropolis newspaper, 25, 51, 52, 71, 89, 96, 97, 123
Florida Times-Union newspaper, 15, 19, 20, 21, 23, 27, 28, 29, 32, 40, 41, 45, 57, 67, 68, 69, 70, 77, 78, 79, 83, 84, 102, 103, 108, 109, 111, 114, 116, 124, 127
Fort Meyers, Florida, 108
From the Manger to the Cross (film), 32

Garrick, Richard, 109, 112, 114, 121
Garrick Studios, 55, 57, 96, 109, 112
Gaumont Players, 109, 112, 121
General Film Company, 35–36, 40, 46, 52, 54, 58

"Get Rich Quick Wallingford" series, 42, 52
Gillstrom, Arvid E., 54, 60–66, *61*

Ham and Bud comedies, 34–35, *34,* 38, 90
Hardy, Oliver Norvell "Babe", 21, 27, 41, 42–43, 44n3, 46, 47, *48,* 52, 54, 55, 56, 61, 62, 63, 66
Hiers, Walter "Fatty", 79, *80,* 82–83, 85, 91
Hitchcock, Frank H., 58
Hotaling, Arthur D., 41
Howell, William A., 15, 25, 75, 79, 82, 83, 85, 87–88, 94
Hotel Mason, 16, *17,* 18, 21, 23, 27, 78, 97

Jaxon comedies, 54, 56, 58, 113

Kalem Comedies, 15, 18, 28–39, *33, 34, 37,* 40, 58, 75, 82, 90, 100, 108, 111, 112, 121
Kennedy, Mary, 34, 38
King-Bee Films Corporation, 54, 60–66, *63, 64, 65,* 113
Kleine, George, 28, 58, 90
Klutho, Henry John, 100, 126
Klutho, H.J., 100
Klutho Studios, 100–103, *101*, 113, 126
Kremer, Victor, 103

Lambert, Glen, 100, 102
Lawrence, Ed, 36
Long, Samuel, 28, 32
Lubin comedies, with Oliver Hardy, 41–43, 52, 56
Lubin Film Company, 40–43, 45, 46, 51, 52, 56, 57, 58, 79, 85, 90, 102, 112, 121
Lubin, Siegmund, 40

Majestic-Punch Comedy Company, 104
Marion, Frank K., 28, 32, 36

Martin, John W., 114, 116, 117, 118, 120, 121, 122
McKee, Ray, 56
McNish, Frank, 86, 87, 93
Melville, Rose, 29–36, 112
Miles Brothers Motion Picture Company (San Francisco), 59n1
Minsey, Frank, 36, 38
Minsey, Frank, 36, 38
The Morning Telegraph newspaper (New Rochelle, NY), 75, 78
Moore, W. Eugene, 25, 78, 82, 83
Murdock, Henry, 34, 38
Museum of Science and History, 127
Myers, Harry C., 47, 52, *53,* 54, 56, 104

Nelson, Richard Alan, 103n3, 121, 126
New Jersey, 45, 60, 66, 87
New York City, 14, 15, 28, 41, 42, 45, 58, 59, 60, 66, 71, 87, 95, 100, 104, 113, 126
Novelty, 42

Old Arlington, Inc., 126
Oscar and Conrad comedies, 87, 94
Ostrich Farm, 104, *106, 107,* 108

Park Theater, 108, 109, 112
Pathe, 42, 58, 86, 90
Peck, Frederick S., 58–59
Perez, Fernando, 46, 56, 104, 113
Plump and Runt comedies, 46, 47, 52, 54, 55
Pokes and Jabbs comedies, 46, 47, 54, 55, 58
Purdon, Richard, 34, 38

Riverside Avenue, 32, 40, 41, 45, 46, 47, 55, 58, 60, 111
Roseland Hotel, 32, *33*

Santa Monica, California, 32, 112
Screen Club of Jacksonville, 27
Seminole Hotel (Jacksonville), 16, 23, 26, 70, 110, 113

Sis Hopkins comedies, 28, 31, 32, 34, 38
Sparkle comedies, 54, 58
St. John's River, 32, 40, 57, 68, 108
Star Light, 42
Stull, Walter, 46, 47, *50, 51,* 51, 54, 55, 58, 63

Talleyrand Avenue, 104
Thanhouser, Edwin, 74–91, 113
Thanhouser Film Company, 74–91, *75*
Theby, Rosemary, 47, 52, *53,* 54, 56
Tom Mix westerns, 108
Tracey, Bert, 46, 47, 52

Tweedledum and Tweedledee comedies, 71–73

United States Film Corporation, 102, 111
Unity Sales Corporation, 71, 72

Vim Comedy Company, 42, 45–58, *48,* 60, 72, 104, 111, 113

West, Billy, 54, 60–66, *63, 64, 65,* 103
Windsor Hotel (Jacksonville), 23, *24, 25*
World War I, 14, 36, 74, 99, 104, 112, 113, 121, 122

www.ingramcontent.com/pod-product-compliance
Lightning Source LLC
Chambersburg PA
CBHW051814230426
43672CB00012B/2727